Religion without Explanation

A

D. Z. Phillips

Religion without Explanation

BASIL BLACKWELL / OXFORD

© Basil Blackwell 1976

British Library Cataloguing in Publication Data

Phillips, Dewi Zephaniah
    Religion without explanation.
    Bibl.–Index.
    ISBN 0–631–17100–2
    1. Title
    200′.1   BL51
    Religion–Philosophy

Set in Spectrum
and Linotype Juliana
Printed in Great Britain by
Western Printing Services Ltd, Bristol
and bound at
The Kemp Hall Bindery, Oxford

Contents

To Aled, Steffan and Rhys

Preface

It might be helpful to say a word at the outset about the plan of this book. I take as my starting point the enormous influence Hume has had on contemporary philosophy of religion. His emphasis on the one world in which we live and move and have our being, and his thorough-going attack on attempts to infer the existence of God from that world or features of it, have given to us a philosophical legacy we cannot ignore. Many influential thinkers who became inheritors of this legacy, directly or indirectly, tackled the problem of what account can be given of religious beliefs if one accepts the force of Hume's arguments. They came to the conclusion that religious beliefs are the product of elementary mistakes due to a primitive mentality, emotional stress, or social pressure. I attempt to examine these views and come to the conclusion that they suffer from many conceptual confusions. I reach these conclusions by appeal to the use which language has in many religious beliefs. I argue that it would make no sense to call these beliefs mistakes, which is what the various explanations I consider make of them. It is important to realize that this conclusion is reached, not in order to protect these religious beliefs, but to show their character. Yet, it is insufficient to say that because it makes no sense to call a belief a mistake that that belief could not be confused. All confusions do not take the form of mistakes. This is true of metaphysical conclusions. I argue, however, that there is very little analogy between religious belief and metaphysical belief.

It is important to recognize that, given its assumptions, Hume's attack on certain theistic arguments is entirely successful. It is equally important to see that many forms of religious belief are free from these assumptions. This may not be apparent always, hence my taking as an example, belief in the reality of the dead, a belief which would seem subject to Hume's severest strictures. In showing other possibilities of religious belief, the charge of reductionism may be made against the attempt. I try to show why this charge is unjustified.

If Hume has had an enormous influence on philosophy of religion, I think the influence of Ludwig Wittgenstein, if less direct, is of equal importance. I try to show this in the following context: For much of the book I have discussed those who wanted to find explanations of religious belief. In the concluding chapters I compare them with those who wanted explanations in other spheres of philosophy. The comparison is more striking than one might think at first. Just as there are unquestionable propositions in certain contexts, such as our talk of physical objects, so, I argue, there are, in one sense, unquestionable beliefs in religion. This is why religion must remain, in a way I try to make clear, without explanation. Of course, an account must also be given of how, despite this fact, it makes sense to criticize, rebel against, and reject, religious belief. In this work, theoretical theism and theoretical atheism are rejected, so that we may reach a clearer understanding of what it means to believe or not to believe in God.

In anticipation of my critics I ought also to say a word about the title I have chosen for this book. When I say that religion can do without explanation, the explanations I have in mind are those which I discuss in various chapters: explanations which seek to characterize religious belief as the false or confused result of ignorance, emotional stress, social pressure or metaphysical impulse, or explanations which seek foundations for faith in philosophical arguments or proofs. If it be said that in showing this I have myself explained something about religion, I have no objection. Neither do I have an objection to calling certain forms of elucidation explanations, although in the text I have kept them apart. For example, in art appreciation one painting may be put alongside another to bring out a deeper treatment of a common theme. These forms of explanation, if one insists on calling them that, are not those which characterized the rationalistic traditions which have had such a widespread influence on the philosophy of religion.

This book grew out of lectures given over the last six years at the University College of Swansea in a course called Religion and Explanation. During these years I have benefited from discussions with colleagues and students at Swansea and at various philosophical societies. In particular, I should like to thank Donald Evans and Ilham Dilman who read the whole work and made many valuable suggestions and criticisms. I should also like to thank the Secretaries of the Department of Philosophy, Mrs. Valerie Gabe and Mrs. Margaret Williams, for helping me with the typing of the manuscript.

Swansea, September 1975   D.Z.P.

Do not all charms fly
At the mere touch of cold philosophy?
There was an awful rainbow once in heaven:
We know her woof, her texture; she is given
In the dull catalogue of common things.
Philosophy will clip an Angel's wings,
Conquer all mysteries by rule and line,
Empty the haunted air, and gnomed mine—
Unweave a rainbow . . .
John Keats

Our hearts are thrilled with compassion, for it is old Jehovah himself
who is making ready to die. We have known him so well, from his
cradle in Egypt where he was brought up among the divine
crocodiles and calves, the onions and ibises and sacred cats ... We
saw him bid farewell to those companions of his childhood, the
obelisks and sphinxes of the Nile, to become a little god-like king in
Palestine to a poor nation of shepherds. Later we saw him in contact
with the Assyro-Babylonian civilization; at that stage he gave up his
far-too-human passions and refrained from spitting wrath and
vengeance; at any rate, he no longer thundered for the least trifle ...
We saw him move to Rome, the capital, where he abjured everything
in the way of national prejudice and proclaimed the celestial equality
of all peoples; with these fine phrases he set up in opposition to old
Jupiter and, thanks to intriguing, he got into power and, from the
heights of Capitol, ruled the city and the world, *urbem et orbem* ...
We have seen him purify himself, spiritualize himself still more,
become paternal, compassionate, the benefactor of the human race, a
philanthropist ... But nothing could save him!
    Don't you hear the bell? Down on your knees! The sacrament is
being carried to a dying God!
Heinrich Heine

A religious symbol does not rest on any *opinion*.
Ludwig Wittgenstein

Do you think there *must* be a significance, an explanation? As I see
it there are two sorts of people: one man sees a bird sitting on a tele-
graph wire and says to himself: 'Why is that bird sitting just there?',
the other man replies 'Damn it all, the bird has to sit somewhere.'
An Examiner's remarks related by M. O'C. Drury

One

Introduction: Faith and Philosophical Enquiry

To anyone reading widely in contemporary philosophy, philosophy of religion must appear, in many respects, to be a branch of the subject which is very much an exception. First of all, to call it a branch of the subject might be going too far for many philosophers, since the bestowing of the title might be taken to assume the reality of the object of the investigation, namely, God. Whatever differences may exist between philosophers who discuss what it means to know something, few if any would deny that we do have knowledge of many things. Similarly, despite philosophical differences about what ought to be said about the reality of material objects, few, if any, would deny the reality of such objects. Again, philosophers may give widely differing accounts of scientific, historical, moral, aesthetic or political judgements, but few would deny that there are realities with which science, history, morality, art and politics concern themselves. In connection with all these activities philosophers might well want to distinguish between practical doubt and philosophical doubt.

There are familiar ways in which we can illustrate the way in which practical doubt gets a hold on us. Having heard of the heavy bombing on Swansea during the last World War someone who has not visited Swansea since then might say, 'I doubt whether St. Mary's church still exists'. Or again, if I am driving in a fog I may doubt whether it is a tree that looms up before me or simply a tree-like shape caused by the swirling fog. One could go on enumerating examples of this kind. The point is clear enough: in unfavourable conditions of various kinds we may have good reason to doubt the existence of particular material objects. The doubt is an understandable doubt. The doubt also has certain practical consequences. If I doubt whether St. Mary's exists I shall view with suspicion an appeal for the fabric fund. If I doubt whether it is a tree before me in the fog I shall proceed with caution rather than swerve unnecessarily.

On the other hand, when the philosopher says that he doubts the existence of material objects, the situation seems odd. The philosopher's doubt does not arise in the context of practical uncertainty. In the examples we have mentioned, the uncertainty is explained in terms of certain circumstances. In the absence of these circumstances the uncertainty could be dispelled. A trip to Swansea would settle the doubt about the existence of St. Mary's and doubts concerning the tree would lift with the fog. But the philosopher's doubts cannot be settled in this way. The philosopher doubts the reality of St. Mary's and the tree even when he is confronted by them! Nothing can be appealed to in order to settle this doubt since the philosopher is doubting in the presence of those very things which one would normally appeal to in settling practical doubt. The difficulty is too see how philosophical doubt can gain a foothold, how it makes a difference to anything. To bring out this odd characteristic of philosophical doubt, it has been called pseudo-doubt. Yet, it would be misleading to say that philosophical doubt goes too far; to characterize the philosopher, as one might the neurotic doubter, by saying that he goes on doubting long after reasonable men have resolved the question to their satisfaction. This is because the objector assumes that philosophical doubt is an excessive extension of practical doubt. He assumes that the two kinds of doubt are of the same kind. This is his mistake. When the philosopher doubts whether St. Mary's church is real, even when he is standing in front of it, his doubt is not a practical doubt. He is not doubting whether St. Mary's exists, but he is doubting whether an intelligible account can be given of what it means to say that St. Mary's does exist. A man may be quite sure that St. Mary's does exist and yet be extremely puzzled about what it means to say that he knows this or that he believes this. If he is a philosopher he may differ widely from his colleagues in the account he gives of these matters and yet, at the same time, along with them, find no difficulty in locating St. Mary's or in directing others to it. These practical activities go on unaffected by the philosophical speculations about them.

Eventually the same points, suitably modified, can be made about morality and politics and the other examples I mentioned. The modification is called for because in this context one cannot make such a sharp distinction between practical and philosophical doubt. Although philosophical analyses of moral and political concepts can be distinguished from the holding of moral and political points of view, there is little doubt that the analyses themselves have often influenced the content and development of the points of view. Even so, this is still far from any suggestion that a philosophical analysis of what it means to hold moral or political views can itself be equated with the establishing of a moral or political point of view. An analysis may operate negatively at times in revealing confusions in certain points of view, but even then it is extremely doubtful whether the values associated with them will not survive the exposure of these confusions. So in this context too the practical activity of making moral and political judgements can be distinguished from the philosophical arguments concerning the meaning of such judgements.

When we turn from these spheres to the philosophy of religion the situation seems radically different. In the previous examples we have considered we have seen that whereas philosophers may differ in the philosophical accounts they offer, none of them denied, outside philosophy, the reality of what they were investigating. This is not the case where the question of God's reality is concerned. Here, philosophers are divided over the question whether there is a God, not only within philosophy, but outside philosophy as well. Of course, this reflects a wider difference between the spheres being investigated. No one denies the existence of material objects. Despite all their differences, no one denies that there are moral and political values. What people make of them is another matter. Yet, where the question of God's reality is concerned, it is a fact that not all people recognize that one is talking about any kind of reality here. It is not surprising, therefore, to find that unlike any other branch of philosophy, many philosophers still think that in relation to the question of God's reality, the primary task of philosophy is to settle it one way or another. Here, there seems to be no difference between philosophical and practical doubt. I do not think this issue is affected by the distinction which can be drawn between those philosophers who think that although it makes *sense* to say that there is a God, there is no God, and those philosophers who think that to speak of God's reality is meaningless, since in both cases the result is atheism.

Yet, despite the fact that the picture I have given of the differences between the philosophy of religion and other branches of philosophy still dominates contemporary philosophy of religion, I believe that the picture is a highly misleading one. It contains far too many unexamined assumptions about the relation between religious belief

B

and philosophical enquiry. If these assumptions are examined, I believe that the differences between the philosophy of religion and other branches of the subject would be seen to be illusions and that philosophy in this context too would be seen to be neither for nor against religious belief. Its task would be seen to be a descriptive one: that of bringing out the kind of language involved in religious belief and the notions of reality embodied in it. One of the main purposes of this book is to establish this conclusion.

Many of the assumptions concerning the relation of faith and philosophical enquiry which need examining were made explicit in John Cook Wilson's neglected paper, 'Rational Grounds of Belief in God'.[1] He points out that in the history of philosophy philosophers have been more concerned with asking whether the existence of God can or cannot be proved than with asking whether the subject-matter they were interested in was itself appropriate for such a question.

The relation between the enquirer and proof-seeking in religion may be quite a complex one. One person may feel that there *must* be a proof of the reality of God if only it could be found. When he finds that the proof under consideration is unsatisfactory, he will, in the light of his prior conviction, still go on searching for a proof. He might say that perhaps he is looking for the wrong kind of proof, but remain convinced that there must be a proof of some kind. With another person, things might be very different. He may not admit the possibility of any proof of the existence of God, so whichever proof is offered will be unsatisfactory. A third possibility is one where the religious conviction is held prior to any proof, but then an urgency is felt about securing a proof. The proof finally obtained may be a faulty one, but the desire to retain the conviction is so strong that it blinds the believer to the flaws in the proof. Furthermore, he even comes to feel that without the proof something essential would be lost. In this way a paradoxical situation comes about: proofs come to be thought of as essential for something which was known before the proofs were devised. A fourth possibility is one in which no flaw in a given proof can be detected. Nevertheless, the proof is felt to be inadequate, the reason being that it seems too neat, too theoretical. The proof does not touch our feelings and as such seems removed from the very thing it was supposed to be a proof of: the reality of God. The perceptive character of Cook

Wilson's paper can be seen in the fact that the four possible attitudes to proofs of the existence of God that he outlines can all be found at work in contemporary philosophy of religion. His paper provides a framework within which these different attitudes can be understood.

The same conclusion can be drawn about two radically different points of view which stem from a question concerning religious belief which is closely related to the request for proofs: the question of whether religious beliefs are reasonable. When we search for the rational basis for an activity this is often an indication that that activity is suspect in our eyes. We do not ask for the rational basis of activities which we do not suspect in this way. To use Cook Wilson's example: we do not ask whether medicine has a rational basis, but we do ask whether faith-healing has a rational basis. It is important to emphasize that we seem able to think of the activity in question independently of the so-called rational basis.

Yet, these facts provoke two very different reactions where religious belief is concerned. The first reaction is to say that religious belief does and does not have a rational basis. It does not have a rational basis if by this is meant that the activity must be accepted on its own terms. It does have a rational basis if by this is meant that the activity can be explained rationally. By bringing the religious activities under the scope of the appropriate rational context, they can be explained. Of course, such explanations will show us that religion is not what its adherents took it to be. This is a reaction which we shall meet many times throughout this book. Time and time again we shall find thinkers insisting that one must distinguish between what religious believers think they are doing and what in fact they are doing. 'The Greeks sought, for example, a rational basis for the phenomenon of thunder and lightning, which had been assigned to Jupiter, and supposed they found it in the quenching of fire, and this does away with the non-natural basis' (p. 842). By bringing the religious belief under a rational system one dispenses with the need for it. In providing such rational systems the early anthropologists and psychoanalysts were markedly different from contemporary philosophers of religion. Many philosophers will say that religious believers are guilty of conceptual confusion; that words cannot be used in the way in which religious believers want to use them. One cannot say that God exists necessarily because to speak of necessary existence is a contradiction in terms. One cannot speak of a loving God, since if one describes someone as loving one must allow, in principle, at least, that something should be able to count against so describing him. And so on for a hundred instances. It follows, these philosophers would argue, that whatever religious believers are doing, they cannot be doing what they think they are doing. Such philosophers might well argue in the following way:

> Our reason has a right to call every belief in question, to ask for and criticize the evidence for them. Religious beliefs will not really stand this test. To conceal the weakness Theology tries to avoid the attacks of reason by taking refuge behind mysteries. It assumes a mysterious source of religious truth, Revelation, and a mysterious faculty of religious truth, Faith; and, the more effectually to put reason out of court, it insists that these are above reason, superior to it and with an authority beyond the canons of reason. (pp. 840–1)

Yet, whereas most philosophers content themselves with displaying the conceptual rules which religious believers break, the early anthropologists and psychoanalysts went further in attempting to tell us what religious believers are doing if they are not doing what they think they are doing. It is odd that contemporary philosophers show no desire to do likewise. After all, such widespread confusion should give rise, and has given rise in others, to a burning curiosity regarding what is going on in these contexts if things are not what they seem. If there is confusion here, it is not trivial confusion. The trouble, if trouble there be, is serious trouble. Hence it is rather comic to receive as a reply to the question, 'What is this man doing when he says he is calling on his God?' 'Misusing language'! Yet, despite the fact that the early anthropologists and psychoanalysts took this question further than contemporary philosophers of religion, they are one with them in their reaction to the question whether religious belief has a rational basis. If by this question one is asking whether the beliefs can be taken at face value, the answer is No. If, on the other hand, one is asking whether the beliefs can be explained away as forms of confusion, the answer is Yes.

The second reaction to the question whether religious beliefs have a rational basis could not be further removed from one we have just been discussing. Here, so far from bewailing the fact that no such basis can be found, the independence of religion from reason is celebrated as a sign that such activities have a higher basis than reason. We may come to see that religion does lack what has already been defined as a rational basis. This is not to say that it has no basis, but simply that it lacks the kind of basis that is called rational. Furthermore, we may conclude that the basis it has is the only kind of basis religion could have. To say this is not to take anything away from the reality of religion, or to impute some kind of inferior reality to it, but rather, to recognize the kind of reality that religion has.

Again, the perceptive nature of Cook Wilson's paper can be seen from the fact that the two reactions he outlines now dominate contemporary philosophy of religion. The consequences of philosophical enquiry about religion according to the two reactions are, of course, very different. According to the first, religion has a rational basis which is unrecognized by believers. When the basis is recognized the believers can no longer continue to believe, because they can now see that their beliefs are not what they took them to be. According to the second reaction, we come to recognize, through an investigation of religious belief, that it does not conform to the paradigm of rationality which has been laid down as a norm. In saying that religion may have a basis which is different from a rational basis, Cook Wilson was not suggesting that religious belief is irrational. His point could be expressed more clearly if we said that through an investigation of various human activities associated with science, religion, morality, art, politics, etc., one may be brought to see that there is no one paradigm of rationality to which all human activity has to conform. At least at this stage of our enquiry the philosopher cannot *assume* that there is one paradigm of rationality. If there are different basic features of human activities then it may be true of religious belief that 'in fact the possibility of a "non-rational" basis will be exactly characteristic of such a belief compared with those which have a rational basis only; and it is obviously to the distinguishing characteristic that scientific or philosophic investigation must be directed' (p. 842).

If through such investigation we are brought to see the kind of thing religious belief is, it does not follow that we shall have been given anything like a philosophical demonstration of the truth of religion. In showing the kind of thing religious belief is, one is not advocating belief in it. On the contrary, the investigation is as essential to an understanding of atheism and rebellion as it is to an understanding of religious belief. More than anything for the philosopher, however, the investigation is a clarification of the nature of activity which has almost always been an important feature of human life. To achieve such clarification it will be important to be aware of differences between human activities, so that we shall not be too ready to assume that what it makes sense to say of one it must make sense to say of another.

NOTE

1. John Cook Wilson, 'Rational Grounds of Belief in God', in *Statement and Inference.*

Two
Hume's Legacy

To the man not interested in philosophical questions it may seem
strange that men remain puzzled by very many of the questions
which puzzled Plato. He asks why there has not been progress in
philosophy comparable, say, with the progress achieved in the
natural sciences. It is wrong to deny that there has been progress
in philosophy. Yet, however much can be shown of the way in
which the treatment of certain questions has developed over the
years, it remains true that the individual, in one important sense,
must start from scratch. He must do so in the sense that if he is to
be a genuine enquirer he must begin with his own puzzles. Philosophical puzzles cannot be answered on one's behalf by another,
since even if another philosopher sheds light on the problems one
is interested in, one must work through those problems for oneself
if one's puzzlement is to give way to a new understanding. This is
one reason why it does not make sense to speak of the end of
philosophy when all questions would be resolved once and for all.
Every individual who is philosophically puzzled must philosophize
on his own account. Furthermore, there is another familiar feature
of philosophy which makes talk of its coming to an end in the
sense specified a misunderstanding. I refer to the fact that very often
when a person thinks that he has freed himself from the hold of a
conceptual misunderstanding, one need only shift the area of interest
to find that all the old assumptions reassert themselves again. In
addition to this, changes outside philosophy constantly throw up
new philosophical problems, or place the old problems in a new
context such that the way to tackle them is difficult to discover. All
this goes to show that one does not philosophize in a vacuum. One
philosophizes at a certain time and place when some interests and
concerns in the culture at large are more dominant than others. Yet,
despite this fact, the deepest philosophical reflections about these
interests and concerns will always lead us back to the central
questions of philosophy.

These general remarks apply to religion as much as to anything else. Many philosophers would say that religion is not a dominant feature of our present-day lives, but, even if this is true, it is important to ask why this is so. The answer to this question, if it were to be a full one, would be one of great complexity and variety. At the moment I am simply concerned to answer the question from within philosophy, and there, I suggest, the answer has much to do with the legacy of David Hume's philosophy, and, in particular, of his work, *Dialogues Concerning Natural Religion.* Hume's reflections on religion have had an enormous influence and have formed for many who have come after him the essential terms of reference within which philosophical reflection about religion is to be carried on. Whether those who have come after him have been sympathetic to religion or unsympathetic to it, they have for the most part shared the assumption that the problem for any philosophy of religion is of how one can accept Hume on his own terms and still talk about the reality of God. It is important, therefore, at the outset of our enquiries to examine the nature of Hume's philosophical legacy as far as the philosophy of religion is concerned.

Without a doubt, one main feature of Hume's legacy has to do with the problem of how one can infer the existence of God from features of the world within which we live. Of course, we have earlier forms of this argument, notably in St. Thomas Aquinas's *Summa Theologica,* but I shall concentrate on what Hume has to say on these matters. In stating the problem in this way, Hume was reflecting the popular way in which religious beliefs would be defended in his day. I suspect that this kind of defence would still be found to be the most popular today, so it is not surprising to find many philosophers of religion still in the grip of its assumptions.

These assumptions, at a first glance, are very persuasive. For example, when we face the plain fact that some people believe that God created the world and that others do not, that some people believe that the world is governed by a divine providence and that others do not, it seems natural to suppose that one group or the other must be mistaken. It seems natural to ask each group for their reasons for holding such beliefs. At the very outset it seems that the matter could be settled fairly quickly, 'After all,' someone might argue, 'one group can only be right if there is a God. So instead of getting involved in disputes concerning creation and providence, why don't we simply settle the straightforward question of whether

there is a God or not?' Yet, as John Wisdom has pointed out, such
a desire is soon to be frustrated, for how does one find out whether
God exists, whether there is Someone behind it all?

> ... take an old question which has very much concerned people—
> the question 'Did someone make the world?' 'Is there Someone
> behind it all?' This seems as if it could be answered like 'Who
> made this watch?' 'Who laid out this garden?' 'Is there a master
> mind behind all these seemingly disconnected crimes?' But it
> can't be answered in that way. It couldn't be. What I mean is this:
> when you are told that there is someone, God, who brings the
> young lions their prey and feeds the cattle upon a thousand hills,
> it is natural to think that if you watch, perhaps in the hush at
> dawn or at sunset, you will see something to confirm this
> statement. You watch. What d'you see? Antelopes feeding
> perhaps, or zebras come down to drink. A lion springs—with
> wonderful acceleration it is true—but still his own acceleration.
> And if anything saves that zebra it's the way he comes round on
> his hocks and gets going. There are the stars and flowers and the
> animals. But there's no one to be seen. And no one to be heard.
> There's the wind and there's the thunder but if you call there's no
> answer except the echo of your own voice.[1]

As a result of this failure to locate God one may conclude that
those who claim that there is a God, that there is someone behind it
all, are mistaken. This conclusion may be countered, however, by
saying that God is invisible: He is not an object in the world. Once
this reply is given, it assumes that belief in God must be founded
on evidence, on an inference in fact, an inference based on features
of the world about us. It is at this stage that Hume's criticisms have
their point.

Hume argues at different levels throughout the *Dialogues*, but all
his arguments are directed against the attempt to infer the existence
of God from the world we live in. Here is one way in which Hume
characterizes the attempt:

> Look round the world: Contemplate the whole and every part of it:
> You will find it to be nothing but one great machine, subdivided
> into an infinite number of lesser machines, which again admit of
> subdivisions, to a degree beyond what human senses and faculties

can trace and explain. All these various machines, and even their most minute parts, are adjusted to each other with an accuracy, which ravishes into admiration all men, who have ever contemplated them. The curious adapting of means to ends, throughout all nature, resembles exactly, though it much exceeds, the productions of human contrivance; of human design, thought, wisdom and intelligence. Since therefore the effects resemble each other, we are led to infer, by all the rules of analogy, that the causes also resemble; and that the Author of nature is somewhat similar to the mind of man; though possessed of much larger faculties, proportioned to the grandeur of the work, which he has executed. By this argument *a posteriori*, and by this argument alone, we do prove at once the existence of a Deity, and his similarity to human mind and intelligence. (p. 143)

I think that at least three levels of argument of increasing severity can be found in Hume's work. The first form of argument depends on the fact that there is a fundamental ambiguity both in the evidence offered and in the character of the author to be inferred from the evidence. Hume makes much of the fact that in the argument which depends on an inference from what we know of the world about us, we have no means of checking the appropriateness of the inference. As Hume says, it is as if we were seeing, and could only see, one half of a balance. Obviously, we cannot infer with regard to the unseen more than what we can see justifies. And when we do look at the nature we know, do we see the neat order that the Argument from Design would have us believe can be found there? Hume answers the question in words which have by now become famous:

Look round this universe. What an immense profusion of beings, animated and organized, sensible and active! You admire this prodigious variety and fecundity. But inspect a little more narrowly these living existences, the only beings worth regarding. How hostile and destructive to each other! How insufficient all of them for their own happiness! How contemptible or odious to the spectator! The whole presents nothing but the idea of a blind nature, impregnated by a great vivifying principle, and pouring forth from her lap, without discernment or parental care, her maimed and abortive children. (p. 211)

Because of the ambiguity of the evidence one cannot infer any of the infinite attributes of God on the basis of it. The character of the author of such mixed effects would have to be equally mixed, or, at least, one cannot rule out this possibility. Certainly the one mixed nature that we know is no basis for inferring the existence of a God who is infinitely wise and good. One cannot infer perfection on the basis of what we know. On the contrary, as Hume points out, if the hypotheses one can devise about the character of the nature we experience are unavoidably ambiguous and varied, so are the hypotheses one can devise about the character of the author of such a nature. This is the way Philo makes the point to Cleanthes and Demea:

> In a word, Cleanthes, a man, who follows your hypothesis, is able, perhaps to assert, or conjecture, that the universe, sometime, arose from something like design: But beyond that position he cannot ascertain one single circumstance, and is left afterwards to fix every point of his theology, by the utmost licence of fancy and hypothesis. This world, for ought he knows, is very faulty and imperfect, compared to a superior standard; and was only the first rude essay of some infant Deity, who afterwards abandoned it, ashamed of his lame performance; it is the work only of some dependent, inferior Deity, and is the object of derision to his superiors: it is the production of old age and dotage in some superannuated Deity; and ever since his death, has run on at adventure, from the first impulse and active force, which it received from him ... You justly give signs of horror, Demea, at these strange suppositions: But these, and a thousand more of the same kind, are Cleanthes's suppositions, not mine. From the moment the attitudes of the Deity are supposed finite, all these have place. And I cannot, for my part, think, that so wild and unsettled a system of theology is, in any respect, preferable to none at all. (pp. 168–9)

Such is the burden of what I have called the first level of Hume's arguments. Yet, they are by no means the strongest arguments he presents. No matter how much he stresses the ambiguous character of the evidence from which the existence of God is supposed to be inferred, he is still employing the notion of evidence. The evidence supplied by the world of nature is ambiguous, but it is still looked on as evidence. This is true even if one takes this argument a stage

further in the way John Wisdom has in his celebrated parable of the
neglected garden. Here, the evidence is not simply ambiguous. The
point, rather, is that even when confronted by the same evidence,
some will believe in a God and others will not. The issue of whether
there is a God or not does not seem to be an experimental one; it
cannot be settled by appealing to evidence:

Two people return to their long neglected garden and find among
the weeds a few of the old plants surprisingly vigorous. One says
to the other 'It must be that a gardener has been coming and doing
something about these plants'. Upon inquiry they find that no
neighbour has ever seen anyone at work in their garden. The first
man says to the other 'He must have worked while people slept'.
The other says 'No, someone would have heard him and besides,
anybody who cared about the plants would have kept down these
weeds'. The first man says 'Look at the way these are arranged.
There is purpose and a feeling for beauty here. I believe that the
more carefully we look the more we shall find confirmation of
this.' They examine the garden ever so carefully and sometimes
they come on new things suggesting that a gardener comes and
sometimes they come on new things suggesting the contrary and
even that a malicious person has been at work. Besides examining
the garden carefully they also study what happens to gardens left
without attention. Each learns all the other learns about this and
about the garden. Consequently, when after all this, one says 'I
still believe a gardener comes' while the other says 'I don't' their
different words now reflect no difference as to what they have
found in the garden, no difference as to what they would find in
the garden if they looked further and no difference about how fast
untended gardens fall into disorder. At this stage, in this context,
the gardener hypothesis has ceased to be experimental, the
difference between one who accepts and one who rejects it is now
not a matter of the one expecting something the other does not
expect. What is the difference between them? The one says 'A
gardener comes unseen and unheard. He is manifested only in his
works with which we are all familiar', the other says 'There is
no gardener' and with this difference in what they say about the
gardener goes a difference in how they feel towards the garden,
in spite of the fact that neither expects anything of it which the
other does not expect.[2]

I do not want to pursue Wisdom's own development of these questions.[3] Within the context of his parable, it is clear that the evidence considered does not simply fail to lead to agreed conclusions about the author of nature, but even fails to lead to agreed conclusions as to whether such an author exists. And yet, even here, we are still talking of what nature shows us as evidence, however inconclusive. It is not surprising that this should be so, since Wisdom's disputants are, after all, disagreeing about a garden. Even if the gardener no longer exists we can argue, quite correctly, that there must have been a gardener sometime. A garden implies design and design entails a designer.

When we come to the second level of Hume's arguments, however, we can no longer proceed in this way, for what he now calls into question is the appropriateness of talking of design in nature at all. Philo points out that to speak of planning as a feature of nature is already to be highly selective. If we look around us we do not simply see the results of human thought and planning. We also see the effects of heat and cold and a thousand other causes. Why should planning be selected as the key which explains everything? Part of the answer might be that we are misled by a tempting analogy. We look at nature, but think of gardens. This was Aldous Huxley's view of the reasons for the confusions he found in Wordsworth's later views on nature:

The Wordsworthian adoration of Nature has two principal defects. The first . . . is that it is only possible in a country where Nature has been nearly or quite enslaved to man. The second is that it is only possible for those who are prepared to falsify their immediate intuitions of Nature. For Nature, even in the temperate zone, is always alien and unknown, and occasionally diabolic . . . A voyage through the tropics would have cured (Wordsworth) of his too easy and comfortable pantheism. A few months in the jungle would have convinced him that the diversity and utter strangeness of Nature are at least as real and significant as its intellectually discovered unity. Nor would he have felt as certain, in the damp and stifling darkness, among the leeches and the malevolently tangled rattans, of the divinely anglican character of that fundamental unity. He would have learned once more to treat Nature naturally, as he treated it in his youth, to react to it spontaneously, loving where love was the appropriate emotion, fearing, hating, fighting whenever Nature presented itself to his intuition as being, not merely strange, but hostile, inhumanly evil . . . Europe is so well gardened that it resembles a work of art . . . Man has re-created Europe in his own image. Its tamed and temperate Nature confirmed Wordsworth in his philosophisings.[4]

Once we do treat nature naturally, the analogy between natural phenomena and human artefacts collapses. Hume's arguments challenged the appropriateness of this analogy and the work of Darwin showed how the adaptation of means and ends in nature could itself be explained in terms of natural development and evolution without reference to a guiding intelligence. Norman Kemp Smith sums up the matter in this way:

> The existence of an artificial product is only possible in and through the existence of an external artificer: the natural, on the other hand, is *qua* natural, self-evolving and self-maintaining; that is to say, its form is as native and natural to it as the matter of which it is composed. Indeed the argument is at its weakest precisely in those fields in which it professes to find its chief evidence—the evidence upon which Paley, for instance, mainly relied—the amazingly complex and effective adjustments exhibited in vegetable and animal organisms. The hinge of a door affords conclusive proof of the existence of an artificer: the hinge of the bivalve shell, though incomparably superior as a hinge, affords no such proof; it is as natural in its origin as anything in physical Nature can be known to be.[5]

With this second level in Hume's arguments, the objections to any attempt to infer the existence of God grow far more serious. Not only is Hume saying that the evidence of design is inconclusive, he is saying that it is misleading to speak of evidence of design in these contexts at all. He is telling us to treat nature naturally. If we do so, we shall find that we arrive at our explanations by relating item to item within nature, without having to appeal to any external intelligence. More correctly, doubt is cast on the whole distinction between that which is within the world and that which is outside it, since, despite his open-mindedness about that which is beyond the world we know, which I take to be ironic, Hume is surely telling us that there is only the world we know. The world we know does not depend on another world beyond or other than itself for its intelligibility. In short, we do not need to infer the existence of God to make intelligible the world about us, for it is in that world, and not in Him, that we live and move and have our being.

Yet, it may be objected that this conclusion has yet to be established. All that has been shown so far is that the facts of nature do not unambiguously provide evidence of order and design and that even where patterns in nature are discerned, these can be explained naturalistically without any reference to a designing intelligence. But all this has to do with states of affairs within the universe. What of the universe itself? Surely, in order to account for the existence of the universe itself one needs to postulate a Maker of that universe. Hume is not unaware, of course, of this classical cosmological argument which differs from the argument from design in that it takes as its starting-point, not any specific features of the world about us, but the fact that there is anything at all. Furthermore, Hume has an extremely impressive answer to the argument, an answer which constitutes what I call the Third level in Hume's arguments. It is an answer which applies as much to the cosmological argument as to the argument from design.

Philo points out that when we infer one thing from another we do so on the basis of past experience. We can say 'If X, then Y' only because we have learnt from past experience that given X then Y. X may not be a particular but a class or kind of event, so that of anything which is an X and of anything which is a Y, one can say, 'If X then Y'. Cleanthes wants to compare the universe to a machine, but the crucial question, as Philo points out, is whether talk of the universe as a whole can be compared with talk of machines, or indeed with talk of any particulars or class of particulars one cares to mention. The legitimacy of the inference from the world to God depends on the appropriateness of the comparison. Philo says that when things are within the same species one can make inferences about their behaviour. Thus, from observing blood circulation in a number of human beings, we are prepared to make inferences on these matters about any human being. But if we observed it in frogs, although the inference is highly probable, it is still only a matter of conjecture that the same conclusions can be drawn about human beings.

Cleanthes, however, wants the existence of God to be more than a conjecture. He doubts whether there is a dissimilarity between the

way in which a house implies an architect, and the way in which
the universe implies the existence of its author. Philo asks whether
one can ask questions about everything in the way one can ask
questions about particular things. The second part of the *Dialogues*
ends with his challenge to Cleanthes which sums up these difficulties:

> Can you pretend to show any . . . similarity between the fabric of a
> house, and the generation of a universe? Have you ever seen
> nature in any such situation as resembles the final arrangements
> of the elements? Have worlds ever been formed under your eye?
> and have you had leisure to observe the whole progress of the
> phenomenon, from the first appearance of order to its final
> consummation? If you have, then cite your experience, and
> deliver your theory. (p. 151)

It is extremely easy to underestimate the criticisms Hume makes in
the first and second parts of the *Dialogues*. When he says that the
species within which an inference is made must be the same if the
inference is to be a valid one, he is not making an empirical
observation. He is commenting on a feature of the logic of inference—
the way in which we use the term 'inference'. He is asking whether
such a term can be used intelligibly to talk of what can be inferred
from the character of the universe as such. He is asking whether it
makes sense to ask questions about the origin of the universe, and
he is denying that an analogy with questions about the origin of
particular things will bring any sense to such questions. There are
important differences between asking, 'How did this house come to
be?' or 'How did this machine come to be?' on the one hand, and
asking 'How did the universe come to be?' on the other.

We can make inferences from the existence of houses and
machines to the makers of such things. We know that a particular
house is unfinished because we know what a finished house is. We
can say that someone must have made the house, because for us
this has become part of what we mean by a house. It is an artefact
and therefore it makes sense to infer an artificer. 'How did this house
come to be?' is an intelligible question, but can we speak of the
universe in this way? We cannot say that the universe has been
made by someone because we have no experience of universes which
have been made or half-made or of unfinished universes. Hume's
point is not a purely agnostic one. He is not simply saying that we

can never know whether anyone made the universe. He is questioning the intelligibility of such talk.

One may think that there is a way of avoiding Hume's objections by stressing the uniqueness of the world's relation to God. Instead of being dependent on what is admittedly a problematic inference from world to God, it might be said that we have an intuition of the world's dependence on God. We simply see that the world bears the mark of its Maker. Unfortunately, far from avoiding Hume's criticisms, this argument simply provides another example of the kind of position against which those criticisms were directed. It is true that when we see a maker's mark on one of his products we need not in fact check on whether the maker made this particular product. The important point, however, is that the matter could be checked if we so desired. The question of whether there is a maker is quite independent of the appearance of his mark. Seeing the mark is not a self-authenticating exercise. It is part of a convention by which we recognize who made the given product, but the fact that someone did make it is not simply a matter of seeing the mark, but something which can be checked independently of that fact. The absence of an independent check in the case of the claim that God made the world leads us back to all the difficulties Hume has raised. We have not escaped or answered their challenge.

There are further difficulties about the question, 'Who made the world?' which can be noted.[6] If one asks how the world came to be, one is asking a question that one normally asks of something particular. In the latter case the answer may be in terms of a process or a development. In any case, the answer will have to refer to something other than the existence of that which one is explaining. But when one asks, 'Who made everything?' where is the logically necessary distinction between the explicans and the explicandum? How can we appeal to something other than 'everything' to explain its existence? Furthermore, where the existence of any particular thing is concerned, it always makes sense to suppose that it might not have existed. But does this make sense when one is talking of 'everything'? At first it may seem to make perfectly good sense. 'After all,' we might say, 'there might have been nothing at all.' But does *this* remark make sense? Normally, when we use the word 'nothing' we use it relatively. We establish that there is nothing by finding out that something is the case. We know that there is nothing in the drawer because the drawer is empty. But when we try to speak of

C

'nothing at all' in an absolute sense it isn't clear that our words mean anything at all.

Peter Geach has suggested 'that what is in fact essential to the "Five Ways" is something tantamount to treating the world as a great big object'.[7] But we have said enough to show that there are insuperable difficulties in talking about the world as a great big object. When we identify a particular thing, the possibility of doing so depends on the fact that we can distinguish this thing from other things. But if we call the world, 'everything', a thing, how do we answer the question, 'This thing as distinct from what?'

It is also tempting to think of the difference between 'everything' and particular things as one of generality. Thus the world might be thought of as the class of all things. Yet one runs into difficulties similar to those encountered in an attempt to speak of the world as a thing. When one normally speaks of a class of things one can identify the class as being this class as distinct from any other class. But what would be the common criteria which would determine what would belong to the class of things we call 'everything'? It seems confused to think of 'the world' as a term which indicates the most general class to which all particular things belong. Rather, if the term 'the world' is to mean anything it gets its meaning in relation to the kind of unity which particular things have. We speak of the world of science, the world of commerce, the world of sport, the world of literature, the world of nature, and so on. We may also speak of 'the world' to indicate the way in which these activities influence each other. This latter use is illustrated in such remarks as, 'What a varied world we live in.' Such remarks, however, should not mislead us into thinking of 'the world' as characterizing an activity of greater generality. It is not the notion of 'the world' which unites these particular contexts, but rather these contexts and their interactions which give the notion of 'the world' its meaning.

Before turning to look at some of the consequences of Hume's legacy for reflections on religions, there is one other claim on behalf of the cosmological argument and the argument from design that ought to be considered. Those who advocate such arguments often claim that an intellectual imperative forces us in their direction. It might be said that we cannot rest content with explanations of why particular states of affairs are as they are. We need to go further and seek an explanation of why there is anything at all. We have already seen however that there are logical objections which cast doubt on the propriety of such an enterprise. But it may also be suggested that particular explanations of specific states of affairs are inadequate, and that no intellectual satisfaction can be found until a final and ultimate explanation is found in God. All explanations in terms of secondary causes are inadequate and unsatisfactory since whatever cause is offered, further questions can be raised about its cause. If an infinite regress is to be avoided, a cause must be found such that no question arises of asking for its cause. God, it is suggested, is such a cause. Yet, as Peter Geach has illustrated,[8] answers to ordinary causal questions need not be thought of as inadequate or incomplete. The fact that the question of origin can be applied to them does not mean that parents have given their child an incomplete answer to the question of where he came from when they tell him the facts of procreation. The intelligibility of this answer does not depend on a whole series of answers concerning a chain of ancestors. This also illustrates the fact that whether an answer to an explanation is considered to be complete depends on the circumstances in which it is asked and the interests represented in the question. There is no necessity that every answer to the question Why? *must* give rise to a further question. Whether this will be so or not will depend on the circumstances. Sometimes, the insistence on asking further questions is not a sign of commendable intellectual persistence, but of stubbornness and stupidity; a failure to recognize when enough is enough. We all know that it does not take too many questions 'Why?' from a child of a certain kind before the child is told not to be silly!

Intellectual integrity, then, does not lead us inevitably to look for an explanation of all things in God. On the contrary, part of Hume's legacy is the demonstration that even where people have thought there were grounds in the world we know for inferring divine activity as an explanation of them, such thoughts have been the result of philosophical confusion. The world we know does not stand in need of any transcendental hypothesis to serve as its ultimate explanation. The whole notion of a God and another world which we can infer from the world we know is discredited. For the kinds of reasons I have outlined most philosophers, I suspect, would conclude that the whole notion of a reality beyond the world with which we are familiar is confused. They would be prepared to agree with Ronald Hepburn's reaction to this dubious reference to a 'beyond'. Hepburn asks us to

... compare these sentences—'Outside my room a sparrow is chirping', 'Outside the city the speed limit ends', 'Outside the earth's atmosphere meteors do not burn out' and finally 'God is outside the universe, outside space and time'. What of this last statement? The word 'outside' gets its causal meaning from relating item to item *within* the universe. It ... is being extended to breaking-point in being applied to the whole universe as related to some being that is not-the-universe: its sense is being extended to the point where we may easily come to speak nonsense without noticing it.[9]

We can now look back and summarize what I have called Hume's legacy in the philosophy of religion. This legacy has much to do with the three levels of argument he employs in discussing the problematic inference from the world to God. The first level of argument concerned the inherent ambiguity in the facts of nature which prevent us from ascribing a general order and design to it. Because of this ambiguity in the facts one cannot be justified in ascribing to God any infinite attributes of perfection. The second level of argument went further and questioned the appropriateness of talking of the facts of nature in terms of design in the first place. These facts admit of natural explanations and there is no need to evoke the existence of a designing intelligence beyond the world in order to explain them. If one raises the question of how the world itself came to be, the third level of argument calls into question the logical appropriateness of discussing this question as if it were similar to the kinds of questions discussed in the second level of argument. Furthermore, the question itself, in the form it is presented, is an unintelligible one. The effect of these three levels of argument which go to make up Hume's legacy is to make any attempt to infer the existence of God from the world in which we live logically problematic. Its practical effect in the world of nature has been to make us treat nature naturally. Similarly, in the world of human affairs, the explanations sought for will be in human terms. Hume's criticisms constitute a powerful attack on the notion of two worlds, an earthly one and a heavenly one, the latter being the explanation of the former. He is, I believe, an advocate of belief in one world, the world we know; a world in which we find no evidence of the existence of God, and from which we have neither reason nor need to infer a divine reality.

Having drawn these conclusions from the observations of this chapter there is one necessary footnote which must be added. I have not the slightest doubt that Hume, through the character of Philo, is deeply committed to demonstrating the philosophical confusions involved in the cosmological argument and in the argument from design. Yet, what are we to make of the following isolated, but striking remarks by Philo, who, as I have said, can be taken to represent Hume's own point of view? At the end of the tenth section of the *Dialogues* we find him saying,

> In many views of the universe, and of its parts, particularly the latter, the beauty and fitness of final causes strike us with such irresistible force, that all objections appear (what I believe they really are) mere cavils and sophisms; nor can we then imagine how it was ever possible for us to repose any weight on them. (p. 202)

Later in the twelfth section, we find him saying that

> A purpose, an intention or design strikes everywhere the most careless, the most stupid thinker, and no man can be so hardened in absurd systems, as at all times to reject it. (p. 214)

> Kant, whose criticisms of the classical proofs of the existence of God in his *Critique of Pure Reason* were greatly influenced by Hume, nevertheless says of the argument from design that it 'is the oldest, the clearest, and the best suited to ordinary human reason. It enlivens the study of nature, just as itself derives its existence and gains ever new vigour from that source.' (A.623)

Again, Cook Wilson, having listed all the objections to the argument from design and found it to be untenable and inadequate, says that if a man turns from theories to look at the facts,

> Can he help feeling admiration and wonder? Whether it be an illusion or not, the idea of plan and design and choice of means come on us with irresistible force; we cannot shut it out. (p. 846)

Shouldn't we be puzzled by this strange contradiction? Philosophers who can find little intellectual worth in an argument suddenly turn aside from their criticisms to talk of what that argument appeals to as striking us with an irresistible force, as being best suited to ordinary human reason and as something we cannot shut out. Kemp Smith was puzzled by this contradiction in Hume and Kant and he asked, 'How can data, which, when impartially considered, are found to be worthless as evidence of design, suffice for producing an overwhelming *impression* of design?' (p. 117). I think that Kemp Smith is right, not only where Hume and Kant are concerned, but also in the case of Cook Wilson, when he says that 'something is evidently wrong in their statement of the situation'. How is this to be understood?

You will recall that in the Introduction, in discussing the relation between religious belief and proofs for their existence of God, Cook Wilson mentioned a reaction of disappointment even when the person concerned could find no flaw in the proof he possessed. The disappointment was the result of a gap between the character of the proof and the character of the belief in God it was supposed to establish. May not Cook Wilson have fallen into his own trap? He is aware of certain reactions to the world of nature, reactions which are religious in character. When he comes to philosophize about these reactions, however, he thinks, wrongly perhaps, that they must be accounted for in terms of the argument from design. He is not alive to other philosophical possibilities. Kemp Smith offers the same explanation for the contradictions we have noted in Hume and Kant. Answering his question of how data which are worthless as evidence of design can nevertheless yield an impression of design, Kemp Smith says:

> The answer would seem to be that while undoubtedly Nature produces an impression which is overwhelming, the impression is being misinterpreted as an impression of design. Minds which have been moulded upon the anthropomorphic Deistic ways of thinking so prevalent in the eighteenth century, and which in popular religious circles are still so usual, will indeed be apt to interpret the impression in this fashion. That Hume and Kant should have done so shows the extent to which they were still under their influence. Immediately the tension of their thought was relaxed, the accustomed ways of thinking resumed their sway. (p. 117)

There are difficulties in the way Kemp Smith wishes to distinguish between an impression and its interpretation which need not concern us here. His point can be made in an unobjectionable manner by saying that if someone's philosophical outlook is dominated by certain possibilities, even when he is impressed by nature in various ways, he will give a philosophical account of these impressions in terms of the only intellectual possibilities he sees open to him. Yet these possibilities may themselves be inadequate to account for that which he wants to elucidate. May not this be the case with religious reactions to nature and religious beliefs in God as creator of the world? If the beliefs are as Hume describes them, Hume's criticisms are, in my opinion, unanswerable. But what if the beliefs are not as Hume described them? It would not be surprising in that event to find that his criticisms had little to do with such beliefs. One of the questions we shall have to pursue in the course of this book is whether there are possibilities of religious beliefs which are different in kind from those which fall under his criticisms, possibilities of which he was dimly aware when he spoke of certain religious reactions to beauty in nature coming to us with an irresistible force. But we are not in a position to answer these questions yet.

In the main, however, what Hume's legacy shows us is that any attempt to pass beyond the world we know by way of inference is odd, since the inference is logically problematic. Our explanations, like our experience, are necessarily found within the one world with which we are familiar.

The reactions to Hume's legacy have been varied. We cannot take account of them all, but it is now time to turn to a consideration of some of the most influential among them.

NOTES

1. John Wisdom, 'The Logic of God', in *Paradox and Discovery*, p. 10.
2. 'Gods', in *Philosophy and Psychoanalysis*, pp. 154–5.
3. I have done so in 'Wisdom's Gods', *The Philosophical Quarterly*, Vol. 19, 1969, reprinted in *Faith and Philosophical Enquiry*.
4. Aldous Huxley, *Do What You Will*, Windus, 1931.
5. Norman Kemp Smith, 'Is Divine Existence Credible?', in *Religion and Understanding*, pp. 108–9.
6. I have already noted many of these in 'From World to God', *Proc. Aristotelian Soc.*, Vol. LXI, reprinted in *Faith and Philosophical Enquiry*. It is necessary to repeat them here for an adequate account of Hume's legacy.
7. P. Geach and G. E. M. Anscombe, *Three Philosophers*, p. 112.
8. Ibid., p. 111.
9. Ronald Hepburn, *Christianity and Paradox*, p. 5.

Three
Are Religious Beliefs
Mistaken Hypotheses?

We have already emphasized that for those who argue that since the existence of God cannot be verified directly it must be inferred from facts in the world about us, Hume's legacy provides insurmountable difficulties. Hume stresses that any attempt to infer God's existence from that of the world or features of it is logically problematic. Yet, if this is so, what are we to make of religious beliefs? How are they to be explained? They can no longer be accounted for in terms of an inference from everyday facts to transcendental conclusions. The answer to these questions which we are about to consider invites us to admit the logical impropriety of such an inference and to put it aside. Further, it asks us to consider whether religious belief need be understood as being dependent on such an inference. What if religious belief can be explained as a natural phenomenon? Such an explanation would deliver us immediately from the difficulties connected with the problematic inference from the world to the existence of God. Tylor invites us to consider the merits of such an explanation:

> We may hasten to escape from the regions of transcendental
> philosophy and theology, to start on a more hopeful journey over
> more practicable ground. None will deny that, as each man knows
> by evidence of his own consciousness, definite and natural cause,
> does, to a large extent, determine human action. Then, keeping
> aside from considerations of extra-natural interference and
> causeless spontaneity, let us take this admitted existence of
> natural cause and effect as our standing-ground, and travel on it
> so far as it will bear us.[1]

The reason why I turn to a consideration of this early anthropological view is not because I want to present an historical survey of changing intellectual attitudes to religion. That is not my primary interest. The point of such a consideration is philosophical, namely, to enquire whether, if one understands religious beliefs in this way, one is illuminating or obscuring possibilities of meaning. The kind of suggestion that Tylor and Frazer put forward is still one, I believe, which has a hold on popular reflection about religion.

Tylor offered a minimal definition of religion in terms of two beliefs. First, a belief that individuals have souls which survive the destruction of their bodies. Second, a belief in other spirits of various kinds which includes belief in the simplest spirits and beliefs in the most powerful deity. These beliefs, however, are not to be taken at face value. They constitute data awaiting explanation. They are the products of human invention. Tylor says that 'as to the religious doctrines and practices examined, these are treated as belonging to theological systems devised by human reason, without supernatural aid or revelation, in other words, as being developments of Natural Religion' (p. 427). That being assumed, it is obvious that the next step is to enquire into the reasons why human reason needed to devise such theological systems. Note the way in which Hume's legacy has influenced this intellectual position. The problem is no longer that of moving, via argument, from evidence of design in nature to the existence of God, but of showing how a belief in God is the product of human design. Tylor's suggestion is that beliefs about the existence of spirits and gods came about by men creating them in their own image. The beliefs are the product of fear, ignorance, and mistaken assumptions about causal connections.

The familiar anthropological story is roughly this: In his early days man found himself in a world that he could not understand, ignorant of the natural causes at work in the world about him. Despite this he was acquainted with some elementary connections between cause and effect in relation to his own bodily movements and effects of those movements. But what of the regularity of the seasons, rain and sun, thunder and lightning, night and day, birth and death? These were things outside his power. Yet, in order to make these strange events less frightening, primitive man reasoned that if no human could control such things they must be controlled by spirits more powerful than himself. In this way primitive man tried to make events in the animal and inanimate world intelligible by interpreting them in terms of his own experience. In this respect Tylor accepted Hume's view:

There is a universal tendency among mankind to conceive all

beings like themselves, and to transfer to every object those qualities with which they are familiarly acquainted, and of which they are intimately conscious . . . The unknown causes, which continually employ their thought, appearing always in the same aspect, are all apprehended to be of the same kind or species. Nor is it long before we ascribe to them thought and reason, and passion, and sometimes even the limbs and figures of men, in order to bring them nearer to a resemblance with ourselves.[2]

We may be sceptical as to whether men would in fact fall into this trap, but Tylor stresses that we are dealing with an early stage in human development. He says that 'Our comprehension of the lower stages of mental culture depends much on the thoroughness with which we can appreciate this primitive childlike conception, and in this our best guide may be the meaning of our own childish days' (p. 478). Tylor mentions the ways in which children tend to be afraid of their dreams and to ascribe real characteristics to their toys.

The above context must be kept in mind, for example, if one wants to understand magical beliefs, according to Tylor. For him, magical beliefs belong to the lowest stages of culture. Their possibility depends on the fact that primitive man does not fully grasp the character of causal connections. He is ignorant enough to confuse a connection in thought, an ideal connection, with an empirical causal connection, a real connection. Such confusions are essential in explaining how magic managed to impress people. They are essential, for example, to what Frazer called contagious magic, the belief that by acting on something closely connected with a person—his property, clothes he has worn, cuttings from his nails or hair—one can bring about one's purposes with respect to him. They are also essential to what Frazer calls homoeopathic or imitative magic, where the connection between the spell and the person to be affected is symbolic or based on analogy. The Zulu chews a piece of wood in order to soften the heart of the man he hopes to buy oxen from. Tylor is in no doubt that all the examples of magic he considers are superstitious:

Looking at the details here selected as fair examples of symbolic magic, we may well ask the question, is there in the whole monstrous farrago no truth or value whatever? It appears that

there is practically none, and that the world has been enthralled
for ages by a blind belief in processes wholly irrelevant to their
supposed results, and which might as well have been taken just
the opposite way. (p. 133)

Again, one might wonder why the world has been enthralled for so
long by complete irrelevancies. Tylor replies that 'If it be asked how
such a system could have held its ground, not merely in independence but in defiance of its own facts, a fair answer does not seem
hard to find' (Vol. I, Ch. IV, p. 133). First, the magician was not
entirely dependent on his art. He made use of natural remedies and
poisons to achieve his ends. He was also a shrewd observer of human
characteristics, for example, signs of guilt. Second, he owed a great
deal of his success to chance and good luck. Third, even in the case
of the large proportion of failures, there were inbuilt explanations
for them within the system. For example, the odds of success could
be improved by the fact that a range of different consequences could
be seen as fulfilments of the same prophecy. It was also possible to
blame the failure on the impurity of the supplicant or on the
interference of a rival practitioner. One could say, in the event of
failure, that the spell had not been strong enough, and if tempest
came instead of fine weather, that the tempest would have been
worse without the spell! Fourth, and most important of all in Tylor's
eyes, is the low level of intelligence in the people we are dealing
with. They are like people in a lottery; the losses do not count for
them. We should not find this hard to believe because the same
tendencies have not disappeared even among the educated in our
culture. How few, Tylor argues, have really taken to heart the
memorable passage at the beginning of Bacon's *Novum Organum*:

The human understanding when any proposition has been once
laid down (either from general admission and belief, or from the
pleasure it affords), forces everything else to add fresh support and
confirmation; and although most cogent and abundant instances
may exist to the contrary, yet either does not observe or despises
them; or gets rid of and rejects them by some distinction, with
violent and injurious prejudice, rather than sacrifice the authority
of its first conclusions. It was well answered by him who was
shown in a temple the votive tablets suspended by such as had
escaped the peril of shipwreck, and was pressed as to whether he

would then recognise the power of the gods, by an inquiry, 'But where are the portraits of those who have perished in spite of their vows?'

Because of these four reasons Tylor concludes that 'On the whole, the survival of symbolic magic through the middle ages and into our own times is an unsatisfactory, but not a mysterious fact' (p. 136).

It is clear that in giving an account of religious and magical beliefs Tylor did not take himself to be simply giving an account of distant practices among so-called primitive men. He finds the same animistic tendencies in the great religions of the world for

> ... as we consider the nature of the great gods of the nations, in whom the vast functions of the universe are vested, it will still be apparent that these mighty deities are modelled on human souls, that in great measure their feeling and sympathy, their character and habit, their will and action, even their material and form, display throughout their adaptations, exaggerations, and distortions, characteristics, shaped upon those of the human spirit. (Vol. II. Ch. XVI, pp. 247–8)

Finally, monotheism is characterized as the final logical development of the early animistic tendencies:

> Among thoughtful men whose theory of the soul animating the body has already led them to suppose a divine spirit animating the huge mass of earth or sky, this idea needs but a last expression to become a doctrine of the universe as animated by one greatest, all-pervading divinity, the World-Spirit. (p. 335)

Furthermore, in his attempt to trace connections between primitive religions and the world religions, Tylor's interest has a reformative aspect. In giving an account of the kind of beliefs magical and religious beliefs are, and revealing the mistakes involved in them, Tylor's enquiry had a missionary zeal. He wanted to lead men from error to the truth, out of darkness into the light. Evans-Pritchard points out that people like Tylor and Frazer were the heirs of eighteenth-century rational optimism. People were bad because they had bad institutions, and they had bad institutions because they were ignorant and superstitious. The way forward has already been demonstrated. According to Frazer men turned from magic to religion because they saw that there was no relation between magical practices and the events which befell them. Instead of thinking that magic powers controlled the elements along with fortune and misfortune, he concluded that some far more powerful spirit must control all these things. In this way, belief in God is born. Man no longer faced a capricious nature, but a God who had reasons for everything that happened, great or small. Naturally, in such circumstances, the reasonable thing to do was to make sure that God was on one's side by obeying His will and offering him gifts. Yet, as time went on, it was obvious that there is as little relation between life's events and religious practices as there had been between such events and magical practices. Man had come of age. He learnt to recognize the real causes of things and to accept what happened to him realistically. He turns aside from all transcendental explanations and treats nature naturally. With this idea of progress as a background, it is not surprising to find Tylor saying:

> To establish a connexion between what uncultured ancient men thought and did, and what cultured modern men think and do, is not a matter of inapplicable theoretic knowledge, for it raises the issue, how far are modern opinion and conduct based on the strong ground of soundest modern knowledge, or how far only on such knowledge as was available in the earlier and ruder stages of culture where their types were shaped. (Vol. II, Ch. XIX, pp. 443-4)

The practical result is that men are freed from the tyranny of dogma, 'religious authority is simply deposed and banished, and the throne of absolute reason is set up without a rival even in name' (p. 450). To achieve an understanding of religious belief, for Tylor, is to achieve liberation from it at the same time. Evans-Pritchard sums up the mood of these early anthropologists as follows:

> If primitive religion could be explained away as an intellectual aberration, as a mirage induced by emotional stress, or by its social function, it was implied that the higher religions could be discredited and disposed of in the same way.[3]

Tylor says as much in the final words of his book:

It is a harsher, and at times even painful, office of ethnography to expose the remains of crude old culture which have passed into harmful superstition, and to mark these out for destruction. Yet this work, if less genial, is not less urgently needful for the good of mankind. Thus, active at once in aiding progress and in remaining hindrance, the science of culture is essentially a reformer's science. (p. 453)

If religious belief does rest on a mistake, analysis marks it out for demolition.

In presenting his account of magical and religious beliefs Tylor did not take himself to be condemning the so-called primitive men who held these beliefs. On the contrary, he holds that 'To impress men's minds with a doctrine of development will lead them in all honour to their ancestors to continue the progressive work of past ages, to continue it the more vigorously because light has increased in the world' (p. 453). Yet, having read what people like Tylor and Frazer have to say about primitive man, do we feel that we are led to them in all honour? Surely, Cassirer is nearer the mark when he says that the picture we are given is one of 'primeval stupidity'.[4] This picture should not be accepted uncritically, however, for there are far-reaching assumptions in these anthropological reactions to religious beliefs, anthropological reactions which have become popular reactions for many people, which must be subjected to philosophical analysis. This is the task which concerns the remainder of this chapter.

The first difficulty is that Tylor's account of religion and magic asks us to believe that so-called primitive men were ignorant of elementary natural facts and elementary causal connections. Surely Wittgenstein is right when he says that 'it never does become plausible that people do all this out of sheer stupidity'.[5] Missionaries and travellers who reported what they saw among these peoples naturally emphasized what to them was strange and bizarre. They did not emphasize what was perfectly familiar in their day-to-day living. Had they done so it would not have been plausible for a moment to accuse the so-called primitives of the kind of ignorance attributed to them by Tylor and Frazer. Herbert Spencer even went so far as to suggest that primitive people had no idea whatever of natural explanation. Yet, as Evans-Pritchard points out, if this were true, it is difficult to see how these people could live at all. In any case, the facts easily refute this suggestion. The peoples concerned possessed considerable technical skills and knowledge. They had a thriving agriculture and, like everyone else involved in such activity, had to take advantage of the regularity of the seasons, the times of the year when sun and rain could be expected, methods of sowing and reaping which had proved successful, and so on. We cannot imagine them engaging in these activities if they were ignorant of natural explanations. They were also skilled hunters. They made their own weapons, knew where to look for their prey and how to stalk it. Again, how could any of this be possible if they were imprisoned by the kind of ignorance ascribed to them by Tylor and Frazer? So, in all these activities they had purposes in view, knew the best means to attain these purposes, and could make necessary adjustments when things did not go according to plan.

Nevertheless, it is true that these activities, which are familiar to us, were often accompanied by other forms of activity which were ritualistic in character. Tylor and Frazer's accounts of magic and religion were offered, in the main, as accounts of these ritualistic activities. We must ask how these ritualistic activities are to be understood. It is important to be clear about the philosophical point of the question. It is easy for the philosophical enquiry to be side-tracked into a dispute over whether an account of a given ritual is correct or not. The discussion then centres around the question whether a particular account of a ritual does reflect what the ritual meant for the people practising it. Such a discussion is justified in so far as the offered account does claim to be an account of the ritual in question, but nevertheless if one does not proceed beyond it the main philosophical issue is obscured. In the accounts they gave of the rituals of primitive peoples, both Tylor and Frazer saw them as supplementations to the purposive activities connected with agriculture, hunting, etc. which we have already referred to. Thus, the *possible* meanings of the ritual were already circumscribed by these assumptions. Tylor and Frazer, I shall argue, were blind to other possibilities of meaning. This is the central philosophical question: whether accounts of what activities *must* mean in order to be intelligible are justifiable; whether it is not often the case that such accounts have a stipulative character, so obscuring from us other possibilities of meaning which do not fit the stipulated paradigm of rationality.

This is what happens, I suggest, when we assume that a ritual connected, let us say, with the harvest, or with hunting, must be related to the goals sought in the same way as sowing, reaping, and stalking the prey are related to these goals. If the same relation were present, one could ask what the ritual is for in the way one can ask what sowing seed at a certain time or stalking an animal in a certain way are for. Tylor and Frazer thought that such a question could be asked and that the answer could be found in certain mistaken hypotheses about supernatural causal connections with the goals pursued. If one accepts this view, one would expect the rituals to serve the purpose of meeting difficulties created by the natural dependencies to which people are subject. How useful it would be if rain could be obtained out of the rainy season, or if a little extra sun could be obtained even when the day has ended. But the rituals do not seem to be used in this way. The following remarks by Wittgenstein bring out this point,

> I read, amongst many similar examples, of a rain-king in Africa to whom the people appeal for rain *when the rainy season comes*. But surely this means that they do not actually think that he can make it rain, otherwise they would do it in the dry periods in which the land is 'a parched and arid desert'. For if we do assume that it was stupidity that once led the people to institute this office of Rain King, still they obviously knew from experience that the rains begin in March, and it would have been the Rain King's duty to perform in other periods of the year. Or again: towards morning, when the sun is about to rise, people celebrate rites of the coming of the day, but not at night, for then they simply burn lamps. (p. 37)

Furthermore, if the rituals are to be understood as causal supplementations to ordinary causal operations, is it not odd that their inefficacy did not become apparent? The attempts made by Tylor and Frazer to explain the fact are not very impressive. Frazer says that

> A ceremony intended to make the wind blow or the rain fall, or to work the death of an enemy, will always be followed, sooner or later, by the occurrence it is meant to bring to pass; and primitive man may be excused for regarding the occurrence as a direct result of the ceremony, and the best possible proof of its efficacy.[6]

Wittgenstein replies,

> Frazer says it is very difficult to discover the error in magic and
> this is why it persists for so long—because, for example, a
> ceremony which is supposed to bring rain is sure to appear
> effective sooner or later. But then it is queer that people do not
> notice sooner that it does rain sooner or later anyway. (pp. 29–30)

If the ritualistic activities are not to be understood in this way, how
are they to be understood? We have seen that the rituals take place
at the same time at which the purposive causal operations we have
mentioned are appropriate. But *must* they be regarded as supplements
to these operations? Is there something called the nature of rationality or intelligibility which forces us to see them in this way? I
think not. The rituals can be seen as a form of language, a symbolism
in their own right; a language and a symbolism which are expressive
in character. Let us consider some examples. The greeting of the
sun at the coming of the day can be seen as a celebration of its
coming. It is not that people who, say, raise their arms at the dawning of day think that unless they raise their hands, the dawn will not
break, but, rather, knowing that the dawning of the day is at hand,
they want to express a greeting to it in this way. Again, why must
the songs and dances before harvest be seen as causally related to its
success? The desires and hopes expressed in this way are expressions
of all that is of value in the occasion. Why must the purificatory
rights before the hunting of an animal and after its death be seen as
causally related to the hunt or to a protection from unfounded fears
of danger? May not these songs and dances be expressions of the
gravity and importance with which the occasion is regarded? Despite
the necessity of the slaying, a life is taken and it must be done with
due gravity and solemnity. When the adoption of a baby is marked
by the woman pulling the child from beneath her clothes, then, to
use Wittgenstein's words, 'it is crazy to think there is an *error* in
this and that she believes she has borne the child' (p. 31). The
ritualistic gesture expressed her attitude to the adopted child: she
will be as close to it as if she had given birth to it. Again, another
example from Wittgenstein's *Remarks*:

> Burning in effigy. Kissing the picture of a loved one. This is
> obviously *not* based on a belief that it will have a definite effect on

D

the object which the picture represents. It aims at some satisfaction
and achieves it. Or rather, it does not *aim* at anything; we act in
this way and then feel satisfied.

One could also kiss the name of the loved one, and here the
representation by the name would be clear.

The same savage who, apparently in order to kill his enemy,
sticks his knife through a picture of him, really does build his hut
of wood and cuts his arrow with skill and not in effigy . . .

The description (Darstellung) of a wish is, *eo ipso*, the
description of its fulfilment. (p. 31)

Wittgenstein is not saying that the savage plunges his knife in order
to express his anger or in order to achieve satisfaction, but that this
is the form which the expression of his anger and satisfaction takes.
Consider one more example. We accompany our dead to their graves.
Does that practice rest on an opinion or an hypothesis? It was once
suggested that this was so. Accompanying the dead to their graves
was the practical means of securing the imprisonment of the dead
and that they would not return to haunt the living, hence the
obliterating of the homeward path. But are there no other possibilities
of understanding here? In accompanying the dead to their graves,
why need one be expressing one's faith in any hypothesis? In
walking to the grave, one may, in the language of gesture, be
showing something about the meaning of life and death. We walk to
the end with a loved one with whom we have walked in life. Is that
any kind of hypothesis? His life is over and the hearth will see him
no more. His footsteps will no longer come to the door, they have
been obliterated from the face of the earth. Is that any kind of
hypothesis? What we see in this ritual is an expression of an
attitude to life and death.

When rituals are seen as expressions of this kind, it can also be
seen that in no sense are they based on hypotheses or opinions. They
are not founded on anything, but express values concerning what is
deep and important for the people concerned—birth, death, hunting,
cultivation of the crops, personal relations, etc. We may not find
these things important in the same way, although there will also be
mythologies expressed in our use of language. This is our privilege.
But we cannot say that the ritualistic expressions were forms of
mistake for that reason. When we see the expressive character of
such rituals, we achieve a clarity about them which the accounts

of Tylor and Frazer would obscure forever. M. O'C. Drury describes
how Wittgenstein's remarks in this context brought him to this
clarity:

> Frazer thinks he can make *clear* the origin of the rites and
> ceremonies he describes by regarding them as primitive and
> erroneous scientific beliefs. The words he uses are, 'We shall do
> well to look with leniency upon the errors as inevitable slips made
> in the search for truth.' Now Wittgenstein made it clear to me
> that on the contrary the people who practised these rites already
> possessed a considerable scientific achievement: agriculture,
> metalworking, building, etc., etc.; and the ceremonies existed
> alongside these sober techniques. They were not mistaken beliefs
> that produced the rites but the need to *express* something;[7] the
> ceremonies were a form of language, a form of life. Thus today if
> we are introduced to someone we shake hands; if we enter a
> church we take off our hats and speak in a low voice; at Christmas
> perhaps we decorate a tree. These are expressions of friendliness,
> reverence, and of celebration. We do not believe that shaking
> hands has any mysterious efficacy, or that to keep one's hat on in
> church is dangerous!
>   Now this I regard as a good illustration of how I understand
> clarity as something to be desired as a goal, as distinct from clarity
> as something to serve a further elaboration. For seeing these rites
> as a form of language immediately puts an end to all the elaborate
> theorising concerning 'primitive mentality'. The clarity prevents a
> condescending misunderstanding, and puts a full-stop to a lot of
> idle speculation.[8]

For Tylor and Frazer, on the other hand, the rites and rituals were
to pass away as men became more rational. Men see the uselessness
of such activities when they come to recognize, to use Tylor's words,
that they have been 'enthralled for ages by a blind belief in processes
wholly irrelevant to their supposed results'. We have now seen,
however, that the rites and rituals can be understood in a way which
shows that they are not meant to be means of producing results in
the way Tylor supposed. This being so, to speak of their irrelevance
for such results simply begs the question. This does not mean that the
rituals cannot lose their hold. It does not follow, however, that the
reason for this happening is that old ways of obtaining certain results

have been superseded by new ways. And yet it is true that an emphasis on more and more effective ways of achieving results could bring about the decline of a ritual. How can this be? Simply by an increased emphasis making the attaining of results the most important thing in people's eyes. Consider, for example, how this could happen, and indeed has happened, where the killing of animals for food is concerned. With more and more emphasis on the killing of animals for trade purposes, profit, etc. it is no mystery to understand how the earlier emphasis on the gravity and solemnity is eroded. Gradually, the ritual is described as a waste of time, irrelevant to the purposes in hand. And as far as the purposes in hand are concerned, this cannot be denied. What has changed, however, are people's ideas about what is involved in killing an animal. Again, consider how the erosion of the ritual of greeting a day could affect people's attitude towards a new day in their lives and the work that has to be performed within it. In face of the erosion of such rituals and the attitudes they express, some people might want to say that in some respects we have lost something worthwhile which earlier people possessed. Others would not agree. Philosophy cannot settle such a dispute. But that is not the point at issue. The point is to see both points of view as *possible* judgements which need not involve philosophical confusion or error. For Tylor and Frazer, however, one of these judgements is necessarily ruled out as an unintelligible point of view. This is because their criteria for what constitutes a rational activity are too narrow, excluding many important forms of language, forms of language which are still with us today, and not only among those who would call themselves religious believers. In the very same breath as he spoke of the need to treat nature naturally Huxley also spoke of a mood of nature as diabolic and of the malevolence of the tangled rattans. To be aware of the mythology in our language we must free ourselves from too restricted conceptions of meaningfulness. Such freedom is a necessary precondition for an understanding of magical and religious rituals.

Another brief illustration of Tylor's positivism can be given in terms of the second characteristic of animism, namely, the belief that individuals have souls. When we speak of matters concerning the souls of men we may be concerned with a wide range of matters concerning people's relationships with one another. We are passing judgement on a person's character when we say that he would be prepared to sell his soul for any menial consideration. A man torn by the worries, cares and troubles of this life may speak of the distress of soul he is suffering. When a person is joyous because of a blessing he has been privileged to possess, he may speak of his soul as raised up in thanksgiving. Others, in expressing how things of the body such as lust and sickness, and things of the world, such as greed and ambition, can warp or destroy the fine things which a person should aspire to, have spoken of the body as a tomb which imprisons the soul. When people want to express how a man's life must be weighed in terms of moral demands which cannot be put aside as matters of whim, desire, convenience or inconvenience, they have spoken of eternal judgement on the soul. Speaking of the sense of a life when it is over, they have spoken of an eternal destiny which the soul of a man enjoys or suffers forever. Such examples could be multiplied, but I hope you get the idea. In all these examples we are talking about a person in a certain way. Talk about the soul is a way of talking about people, a way of talking which, perhaps, is not so familiar as it used to be. What is important to note for our present purposes, however, is that such talk is not based on an opinion or on any kind of hypothesis. It is not dependent on any kind of conjecture about some odd substance inside the body called the soul. Yet, when we listen to Tylor speaking of primitive conceptions of the soul, he speaks of such a substance. He speaks as if the question of whether people have souls is a hypothetical question, an assumption, and, in his view, one which is empirically false and without foundation:

> It is a thin unsubstantial human image, in its nature a sort of vapour, film or shadow; the cause of life and thought in the individual it animates; independently possessing the personal consciousness and volition of its corporeal owner, past or present; capable of leaving the body far behind, to flash swiftly from place to place; mostly impalpable and invisible, yet also manifesting physical power, and especially appearing to men waking or asleep as a phantasm separate from the body of which it bears the likeness; continuing to exist and appear to men after the death of that body; able to enter into, possess, and act in the bodies of other men, of animals, and even of things. (p. 429)

For Tylor, belief in the existence of the soul was the intellectual product of primitive reasoning. The kind of thing he has in mind is clearly very different from the examples where the soul is talked of which I mentioned earlier. Yet, when we turn to the examples Tylor has in mind and which he believes justify his account of the primitive conception of the soul, we find that they are precisely of the kind which characterized the talk about the soul which I illustrated earlier. Referring to his own account of belief in the existence of the soul Tylor tells us that

> ... if any should think such expressions due to mere metaphor, they may judge the strength of the implied connexion between breath and spirit by cases of most unequivocal significance. Among the Seminoles of Florida, when a woman died in childbirth, the infant was held over her face to receive her parting spirit, and thus acquire strength and knowledge for its future use. These Indians could have well understood why at the death-bed of an ancient Roman, the nearest kinsman leant over to inhale the last breath of the departing.... Their state of mind is kept up to this day among Tyrolese peasants, who can still fancy a good man's soul to issue from his mouth at death like a little white cloud. (p. 433)

Thinking of Tylor's understanding of these examples, and of his last remark in particular, one is tempted to repeat Socrates's response to such a positivistic analysis in the *Gorgias* and say that in that case, if the soul is not to be lost, one had better take care not to die on a day when there is a gale blowing!

Tylor thinks that the meaning of his examples are unequivocal and that it is accounted for in his analysis. As a matter of fact, his analysis is more influenced by a philosophical dualism concerning soul and body than by the examples under consideration. The notion of the transfer of power which Tylor sees in the examples is a crude one, almost akin to the transfer of electricity. What Tylor fails to take account of is the significance these gestures have in the relationship between a dying mother and the child she has given birth to, and in the relationship between a dying man and his nearest kinsman. A mother has given her life for her child and this is expressed in the ritual by the child receiving her parting breath. What more needs to be said? In the same way the nearest Roman kinsman receives the parting breath of the dying man and so becomes the heir to an authority and tradition by this symbolic act. Again, these acts are not based on hypotheses or opinions concerning strange invisible substances which, by mysterious means, are transferred from one person to another. On the contrary, the gestures are expressions of something. What they express can be indicated in the ways we have just noted. Ironically, it is Tylor, the rational critic, who is in the grip of the very conception of the soul he sets out to criticize. It is precisely because for him there would have to be a strange substance called the soul in order for the notion to have any meaning that he finds the examples he discusses unintelligible. It is his own positivistic conception of the soul which prevents him from appreciating what the notion may mean in its natural setting.

In conclusion it is important to note that nothing which has been said in this chapter has meant to deny that practices called magical or religious may be shown to be superstitious. One could imagine circumstances where almost all the actions we have described could bear a significance which would merit that description. The point is that there is a wide range of examples where this cannot be said. It is the use of language in such cases which is of particular interest to the philosopher. Why should this be so? I hope the present chapter has illustrated the answer to this question. The use of language is of particular interest because it shows that certain theories about what constitutes rational behaviour are inadequate and too narrow. What is needed, however, is not to replace the narrow theory with a wider one, but to stop theorizing about what conditions must be fulfilled for behaviour to be rational. Instead of stipulating what *must* constitute intelligible uses of language, one should look to see how language is in fact used. If one does, one comes across the use of language found in magical and religious rites and rituals. Such language is not based on opinions or hypotheses, but is expressive in the ways I have tried to indicate. Faced by it, the philosopher's task is not to attempt to verify or falsify what he sees, for that makes no sense in this context. His task is a descriptive one; he gives an account of the use of language involved. He can only say that these language-games are played.

NOTES

1. E. B. Tylor, *Primitive Culture*, p. 3.
2. Hume, *Natural History of Religion*, Sect. ii, quoted by Tylor on p. 477.
3. E. Evans-Pritchard, *Theories of Primitive Religion*, p. 15.
4. See Ernst Cassirer, *The Myth of the State* and *An Essay on Man*.

5. Ludwig Wittgenstein, 'Remarks on Frazer's "Golden Bough"', in *The Human World*, No. 3, May 1971, p. 29.
6. G. S. Frazer, *The Golden Bough*, abridged ed., Macmillan, p. 59.
7. This still sounds too much like an explanation. More strictly the point is that the rites *are* the expression of something.
8. M. O'C. Drury, *The Danger of Words*, pp. x–xi.

Four

Private Stress and Public Ritual[1]

I wonder whether we are content with the conclusions we have been offered so far? If we accepted Hume's philosophical legacy as constituting the necessary context for reflection concerning the character of religious belief, such belief would be shown to be a cluster of logical mistakes. These mistakes come about from not recognizing the problematic character of any attempt to infer the existence of God from features of the world we live in. Once we do recognize these logical problems we can set about explaining how people came to hold religious beliefs. The explanation can be found in the primitive mentality which first devised these beliefs, a mentality which, because of its undeveloped state, put its trust in erroneous scientific beliefs. Such would be one development of Hume's legacy.

Yet, as we have seen, we have had reason to question the terms of Hume's legacy. Hume's conclusions follow only if one important premiss is true, namely, that the traditional proofs of the existence of God are essential to religious beliefs. But is this so? As we have seen, as well as trying to provide rational grounds for belief in the existence of God, the traditional proofs elucidate what they take to be the nature of that belief. In this context a gap opens up between the arguments and the belief, and allows one to conclude that as well as not achieving what they set out to do, the arguments are also inadequate as attempts to elucidate the character of religious belief. The latter conclusion could also be drawn about the attempt at explaining religious rituals we discussed in the last chapter. Such explanations, like the proofs, show an inadequate grasp of the nature of religious belief. We have suggested that where religious belief is concerned, to speak of proof and explanation is to betray a misunderstanding of what is being investigated.

Such conclusions have been welcomed by many who have reflected on religion. Miguel de Unamuno provides one such response:

No one has been able to convince me rationally of the existence of

God, but neither of his non-existence; the reasonings of the atheists seem to me even more superficial and futile than those of their opponents. And if I do believe in God, or at least believe that I believe in Him, it is principally because I want God to exist, and next, because He reveals Himself to me through my heart, in the Gospel, through Christ and through history. It is a matter of the heart.[2]

Yet, such a response has dangers of its own, since some have taken responses precisely of this kind as a starting-point, not for the rejection of Hume's legacy, but for the further development of it and for a further exploration of its implications. How does this come about? To see how, we simply have to pose one all-important question: what exactly is the connection between belief in God and human wishes, how is the heart linked with religion? According to one influential answer to this question, once we come to understand the precise nature of the connection between our desires and religious beliefs, we will give up these beliefs without a second thought. In this and the following chapter we shall examine this view of how religious beliefs can be explained. In the present chapter I shall take R. R. Marett as an example of the point of view I have in mind.

Marett argued that it is absurd to characterize primitive man as an amateur philosopher or as an amateur scientist. This attributes to him a higher mentality than he possessed. More seriously, it obscures the true explanation of his ritualistic practices. Tylor's explanation of these practices in terms of animism is too intellectual in character. No doubt, at some later stage in his development primitive man did people the world with spirits, but the reason why he did so cannot be found in the intellectual mistakes Tylor attributes to him. The explanation is of a more ultimate kind; it lies behind animistic practices and is to be found in the realm of emotions. 'Savage religion', Marett tells us, 'is something not so much thought out as danced out.'[3] We have already seen that according to Tylor and Frazer magic and religion develop because of false ideas about causal connections. By contrast, Marett argues that in such explanations the observer is imposing his own mental capacities on to his picture of primitive man: 'The standpoint of the observer seems to be confused with the standpoint of the mind under observation' (p. 38). Marett, like Wittgenstein, stresses how problematic it is to attribute ignorance of causal connections to these people when their technical activities display a command of causal concepts. He too protests against the foolish light in which Tylor and Frazer's account of primitive rituals places the practitioners:

> How then are we to be content with an explanation of taboo
> that does not pretend to render its sense as it has sense for those
> who both practise and make it a rallying-point for their thought
> on mystic matters? As well say that taboo is 'superstition' as that
> it is 'magic' in Dr. Frazer's sense of the word. We ask to
> understand it, and we are merely bidden to despise it. (p. 84)

Primitive people have causal concepts. They throw a spear and the enemy falls. But when a wizard points a spear and a man falls, some other kind of explanation is called for. Where can such an explanation be found?

Evans-Pritchard tells us that

> According to Marett, primitive peoples have a feeling that there
> is an occult power in certain persons and things, and it is the
> presence or absence of this feeling which cuts off the sacred from
> the profane, the wonderland from the workaday world, it being
> the function of taboos to separate the one world from the other;
> and this feeling is the emotion of awe, a compound of fear, wonder,
> admiration, interest, respect, perhaps even love. Whatever evokes
> this emotion and is treated as a mystery is religion. (p. 33)

This feeling is more primitive than animism, being prior to any distinctions between the personal and the impersonal or between the ethical and the non-ethical. Yet, despite this view, Marett does not want to deny the important place of social institutions in an understanding of religion. Although what he says at other times does not fit in too well with it, Marett stresses that if one's explanations are too individualistic, if one cuts off the individual from society and historical culture, one will end up with mere babblings. Tylor's emphasis on the association of ideas is too individualistic: 'We must say that religion is materialized, incorporated, enshrined, in the corresponding institution or group of institutions' (p. 136). Yet, as soon as he says this, Marett warns that religion cannot be enslaved by its social form. If one simply stresses tradition and custom, what Marett calls the mind of society, one is not taken very far: 'At its best it is the mind of a public meeting, at its worst it is the mind of Babel' (pp. 139–40). Viewed statically, one can give an account of those things, animals and persons, which the primitives regarded as sacred. One can also list the various rituals which surround such attitudes. Social psychology, according to Marett, can take us thus far. Viewed dynamically, however, the same phenomena must be approached via individual psychology. It is in this latter context that the most fundamental question of all is posed: what need do these rituals and customs serve?

Once we answer this question in the way Marett suggests, we see that his explanation of religious rituals, though different in important respects from that of Tylor and Frazer, also has many assumptions in it which are similar to those of their accounts. Primitive man is in a world where much is beyond his control. Not only are death and disease part of every man's lot, but there are purposes and desires which, because of the course of circumstances, remain unfulfilled. This experience of unfulfilment leads to an emotional tension which seeks some form of release. It finds that release in magic and religion. In the mimetic rites, where what is desired is imitated, primitive man convinces himself that what he desires has actually been achieved. Malinowski in *Science, Religion and Reality* follows Marett closely in summarizing this view of magic. Summarizing his view, Evans-Pritchard says:

> Men have inadequate knowledge to overcome by empirical means
> difficulties in their pursuits, so they use magic as a substitute
> activity, and this releases the tension set up between impotence
> and desire which threatens the success of their enterprises. Hence
> the mimetic form of the rites, the enactment of acts suggested by
> the desired ends. (p. 40)

In this way, it is suggested, magic produces the same subjective result as empirical action would have done had it attained its goals, and so confidence is restored.

In order for tension to be eased in the way described, primitive man must believe that there are powers in things, animals and persons which can bring about what ordinary methods fail to achieve. These powers, of course, do not exist. They are products of frustrated desires. In a similar way, fears about unfulfilled hopes and desires lead to the attribution of similar powers which frustrate human

designs. The powers thus attributed are called mana and tabu. Tylor
and Frazer missed all this because they ignored the origin of mana
and tabu in inward experience. Primitive man creates other
possessors of mana in his own image and at this level animistic
assumptions play a role. But the fundamental explanation is to be
found in tensions connected with original impulses in the individual.
Mana and tabu, according to Marett, have no reality. All that is real
are the emotions which gave rise to these beliefs—wrath, anger,
frustration, etc. Marett makes this quite clear as follows:

> Now we need not suppose that because the primitive mind is able
> to explain away its doubts, there is therefore necessarily any
> solid and objective truth at the back of its explanations. Given
> sufficient bias in favour of a theory, the human mind, primitive
> or even civilized, by unconsciously picking its facts and by the
> various other familiar ways of fallacy, can bring itself to believe
> almost any kind of nonsense. (pp. 44–5)

The rituals and rites of primitive men, according to Marett, also
have the function of relieving emotional stress and of providing
conditions for the avoidance of a complete nervous breakdown. He
admits himself that at first this seems to be an unlikely thesis. After
all, there seems to be no correlation between the times at which rites
and rituals are performed and times of natural crisis in the lives of
individuals. Yet, Marett argues, this very fact supports his theses,
since 'it is surely for better rather than for worse that social routine
interposes, as it were, between a man and the brute propensions of
his body' (p. 197). And so we arrive at the full-blown thesis:

> The tendency of pent-up energy to discharge itself along well-worn
> channels or quite at random must be inhibited at all costs; and the
> ritual of *tabu* is, of all the forces of social routine, the greatest
> inhibitor, and therefore the greatest educator, of that explosive,
> happy-go-lucky child of nature whom we call the savage.
> (pp. 197–8)

Rites and rituals do not simply have this negative function, achieved
through tabu. They also have a positive function achieved through
mana. The crises become disassociated from their old physiological
bases by the rituals. Spiritual crises now serve the same role as the

old crises and the rites have a regenerative function. The savage's enforced withdrawal from society from time to time can be understood in this way:

> To cease from active life, and consequently to mope, as it were, and be cast down—such during the early and unreflective stages of religion is no subtle device of the 'higher intelligences', but the normal tribesman's normal way of reacting on a world that is ever making serious and fresh demands upon his native powers. By sheer force of that vital experience which is always experiment, he has found out—or rather society has found out for him—that thus to be cast down for a season means that afterward he will arise a stronger and better man. (p. 200)

The world of nature and human life make tremendous demands on primitive man, demands which, if they became dominant, would bring about a mental and physical crisis. Society eases the threat of such crises through its rituals. One can understand public rituals by realizing that their point is to relieve private stress.

One final point in expounding Marett's views must be noted. Because he explained the function of religious beliefs and rituals, their mystic notions, to use Marett's term, were of secondary importance to him. In fact, they play little, if any, part in the explanations he offers. The form of rituals may vary widely and the ideas involved in them may well cover a wide range, but the explanation of these activities and the beliefs bound up with them is always the same: the public ritual is a way of alleviating and transforming private stress:

> As regards theory, I would rest my case on the psychological argument, that, if there be reason, as I think there is, to hold that man's religious sense is a constant and universal feature of his mental life, its essence and true nature must then be sought, not so much in the shifting variety of its ideal constructions, as in that steadfast groundwork of specific emotion whereby man is able to feel the supernatural precisely at the point at which his thought breaks down. Thus, from the vague utterance of the Omaka, 'the blood pertains to *wakanda*', onwards through animism, to the dictum of the greatest living idealist philosopher, 'the universe is a spiritual whole', a single impulse may be discerned as active—the

impulse never satisfied in finite consciousness yet never abandoned, to bring together and grasp as one the *That* and the *What* of God. (p. 28)

Classifying the kind of explanation of religious belief offered by Tylor and Frazer as an intellectual psychological explanation, Evans-Pritchard helpfully describes the account offered by Marett as an emotional psychological explanation. As in the previous chapter, my purpose in examining Marett's ideas is not historical, but to draw attention to a way of thinking which has influenced the way some people talk of religious belief. Some people talk of religion as the product of ignorance and of outmoded primitive scientific mistakes. Others talk of it as the product of men's emotions, a product of their awe and fear. It is to this second way of talking, using Marett as our example, that we must now turn our critical attention.

There are many difficulties connected with the way of explaining religious belief that Marett represents. The first of these concerns the way in which Marett speaks about emotions as if they were independent of any context. Certain emotions, we are told, explain the genesis of religious beliefs. But what emotions are these supposed to be? Evans-Pritchard points out, rightly, that there is not much point in saying that religion is the product of fear. The generality of such a claim would imply that a man fleeing in terror before a buffalo is performing a religious act. For similar reasons one cannot say that magical rites relieve anxiety and leave it at that, or it will be appropriate to ask why a doctor who relieves a patient's anxiety by clinical means is not performing a magical rite. (See p. 44.) It is sometimes suggested that a priest and an atheist could have the same 'religious' emotion but that their interpretations of it would be different. What leads people to talk in this way? Much of the answer lies in assimilating emotions to sensations. Sensations such as pains, itches, tickles, feeling hot or cold, can be experienced in a vast range of circumstances. Although, of course, one cannot describe anything we like in these ways, it might be said that sensations are, relatively speaking, context-free. But can the same be said of emotions? Can one feel pride no matter what the situation? Can one feel indignant no matter what the situation? Can one feel afraid no matter what the situation? Marett tells us that one purpose of religious rituals is to alleviate fear. But what kind of fear? Men feel fear in a wide range of circumstances: fear of the dark, fear of the consequences, fear of death, and so on. There may be resemblances between these cases, but often the differences between them will be more important than the similarities. It is tempting, but confusing, to think that what the fear essentially consists in is a physical sensation which is essentially the same in all the different circumstances. This can be brought out in terms of a simple example. I may have a sinking feeling while awaiting the results of an interview. I may also have a sinking feeling when I hear the result of the interview announced. Suppose I call the first a feeling of apprehension and the second a feeling of disappointment. How do I distinguish between them? Surely, not by paying close attention to the quality of the sinking feeling. It is not the sinking feeling which teaches us the difference between apprehension and disappointment, but rather, apprehension and disappointment which give significance to the sinking feeling which may accompany them. To speak, as Marett sometimes does, of emotions as physical sensations which explain the genesis of religious beliefs, obscures the internal relations which exist between emotions and their objects. The emotion of pride, for example, must be a response to an achievement, to something that belongs to us in some sense or other—the achievements of one's son, one's football team, one's country, etc. Similarly, the feeling of indignation is a response to the fact that an offence has been committed. Feeling afraid is a reaction to danger of some kind. This is not to say that there cannot be misplaced pride, indignation, or fear, but these exceptions simply prove the rule. A person who feels proud of a magnificent thunderstorm may think that he has had something to do with it! There can only be misplaced pride because there is appropriate pride. There can only be groundless indignation because indignation has good grounds. There can only be fear of nothing in particular because normally we do fear something in particular. If a person only spoke of pride, indignation or fear in these exceptional circumstances we would hesitate to say that he understood the meaning of pride, indignation or fear. Whatever Marett means by awe and fear, it must be awe at, and fear of, something or other. Little sense can be made of his attempt to speak of these emotions as physiological sensations which underlie religious belief.

At other times, as we have seen, Marett is more specific about the emotions which he claims lead to the genesis of religious belief. He speaks of the fear and frustration primitive man feels when his purposes are thwarted. Yet, once something as definite as this is specified, there are further difficulties involved in Marett's view. The point is not to deny that Marett describes a possible relation to religious rituals. A person may come to religion for the reasons Marett outlines. On the other hand, it will always be possible to distinguish between such cases and others which do not fit the description. But this will not do for Marett's case. He is claiming far more than that he is describing some people's reasons for turning to religious belief. He is claiming to give a general account of the genesis of religious belief, such that to understand it is at the same time to understand the essence of religious belief. This claim, however, confuses how a belief may originate with the meaning of a belief. As I have just said, it is not necessarily true that a person does come to a religious belief for the reasons Marett mentions, but even in the cases where this is the case, and even if it could be shown that this is how religion began, it does not follow that what a belief means to a man must always reflect his reasons for believing it in the first place, or that a belief which begins in a certain way cannot develop into something quite different. In order to discover what religious beliefs mean, therefore, one must take account of their place within a tradition of religious teaching and practice. It is obvious that this cannot be accounted for in terms of the motives or feelings of a single individual. Evans-Pritchard tells us why this is so:

> A rite is part of the culture the individual is born into, and it imposes itself on him from the outside like the rest of his culture. It is a creation of society, not of individual reasoning or emotion, though it may satisfy both; and it is for this reason that Durkheim tells us that a psychological interpretation of a social fact is invariably a wrong interpretation. (p. 46)

One must be careful, however, in making this point. Evans-Pritchard is correct in pointing out that the meaning of a ritual does not depend on the state of mind of an individual on a given occasion. The meaning of the ritual is bound up with the history and theology of the religion in question. Yet Evans-Pritchard's point must not be taken to mean that the ritual is independent of all affective states and attitudes. The ritual is itself an expression of beliefs which entail some affective state or attitude. If a ritual ceased to express such states and attitudes it would become cut off from its roots. This is not

E

to agree with Marett, however, since his claim is that the ritual is the *product* of a prior emotional state. What I am saying is that the ritual is not performed in *order* to express anything; it *is* the expression of something. The existence of the rite constitutes the possibility of coming to certain affective states and attitudes—awe, fear, love, wonder, etc., etc. But if one asks what kind of awe, fear, love, wonder, one could only be answered in terms of the religious belief within which they are to be found. That is why Evans-Pritchard says that 'if any emotional expression accompanies rites, it may well be that it is not the emotion which brings about the rites, but the rites which bring about the emotion' (p. 45). This cautious conjecture can be hardened into a point of logic. It is true that one may participate in a rite without thinking much about it, as a matter of routine, but if one does become emotionally involved in the rite, one's emotions will only be intelligible in terms of their internal relation to the rite in question. This is connected with the fact that there is something to learn from a ritual. At first, a person may attend because he does not want to offend his parents. That may remain the case and when he is independent of them he may cease to attend such rituals. It is instructive that when we say here that the ritual simply meant parental enforcement for him, we can also express the matter by saying that the ritual meant nothing to him. Even when a man seeks out a ritual to aid his frustrations, we can still distinguish between what the ritual means to him and the meaning of the ritual. What the ritual means is something he may grow to learn, something quite independent of his early motives for attendance. Indeed, if a person first attends such rites and rituals as a child, it is unlikely that their full significance could become clear at that time. Evans-Pritchard, in criticizing Maret, points out

> ... that in an individual's experience the acquisition of rites and beliefs precedes the emotions which are said to accompany them later in adult life. He learns to participate in them before he experiences any emotion at all, so the emotional state, whatever it may be, and if there is one, can hardly be the genesis and explanation of them. (p. 46)

Thus a child of Christian parents is taken regularly to Holy Communion or to Mass by his parents, and in this sense is introduced to it, *before* the sacrament has acquired any religious significance for him.

Where Marett's description of how a person came to hold a religious belief is true, it could be said that the person is using religion for his own ends. Where a person's state of soul has been created by the religious beliefs he has come to, this cannot be said. This point is difficult to express because religion often does offer solace and consolation. It is important to recognize, however, that what is offered is the solace and consolation of religion. If it is said that Christ offers man consolation and solace, that is different from saying that belief in Christ is the means of satisfying the desire for solace and consolation. It is not that what is meant by solace and consolation in the two contexts must be entirely different, but that the desire for these things prior to religious belief is transformed and redirected within the context of religious belief. The reason why care must be taken in expressing these matters can be illustrated by the following example.

> It is not an explanation of the visions of St. Theresa to say (as Dr. Desmond Morris does, *The Human Zoo*, pp. 87–8) that they merely instance the occurrence of physiologically necessary orgasm among female celibates. She is certainly saying something sexual, and strongly sexual, when she describes her vision of an angel.
>> 'In his hands I saw a long golden spear and at the end of the iron tip I seemed to see a point of fire. With this he seemed to pierce my heart several times so that it penetrated to my entrails. When he drew it out I thought he was drawing them out with it and he left me completely afire with a great love of God. The pain was so sharp that it made me utter several sharp moans; and so excessive was the sweetness caused me by this intense pain that one can never wish to lose it.'
> If St. Theresa does more than dream through some moments and motions of happy (and, for the liberal-minded, beneficial) release, it is because she is making religious sense of what is unavoidably sexual in her life. That is what she is really doing or failing to do, and to that religious sense or failure of sense discussion of her 'religious practices' must address itself. She is trying to weave the sexual and her life otherwise into such a pattern as means that the corruptible shall put on incorruption.[4]

In this example we have but one instance, and a rather remarkable one, of what religion can make of the sexual in a person's life. Not only will there be instances of different significance within the same religion, but different religions may well transform or redirect sexuality in varying ways. Neither can one assume that sexuality itself always bears the same significance in the lives of different people in different cultures. What this shows is the conceptual untenability of Marett's view that the same feelings underlie and explain any conceivable body of religious teaching and practice. There is no single impulse which may be discerned as active throughout these varied contexts. On the contrary, what religion makes of a man's life depends very much on the man and on the nature of the religion in question. To understand how religions have transformed the lives of men one would hardly look at what men have had in store for religion, at the users and manipulators of the Faith whether conscious or unconscious. Rather, one would have to look at what various religions have in store for men and this one cannot do without reference to the ideas and practices involved in those religions. When we look at the particular use which Marett thinks men have for religion, we see that it resides in an answer to human frustration caused by lack of success in their purposive activities. What the world of nature and human competitiveness has denied them, magic makes them believe has been realized after all through occult powers. On this view, religious treasures really are the treasures of this world regained. Yet, when we pass from this view to listen to a deeply religious person speaking of the treasures of this world, the contrast could not be greater. Here are the words of Simone Weil:

> To acknowledge the reality of affliction means saying to oneself:
> I may lose at any moment through the play of circumstance over
> which I have no control anything whatsoever I possess, including
> those things which are so intimately mine that I consider them as
> being myself. There is nothing that I might not lose. It could
> happen at any moment that what I own might be abolished and be
> replaced by anything whatsoever of the filthiest and most
> contemptible sort. To be aware of this in the depth of one's soul
> is to experience non-being. It is the state of extreme and total
> humiliation which is also the condition for passing over into truth.

The truth which Simone Weil is referring to here is the religious belief that nothing belongs to us by right and that everything is a gift of grace. What must be noted for our present purposes, however, is that what she calls the condition for passing over into this truth, is the exact opposite of the condition which, according to Marett, is the reason why men come to adopt religious beliefs and practices. This is but one illustration of the difficulties involved in wanting to analyse religious ideas in terms of a set of needs which they serve and which can be identified independently of them. When such an analysis is accepted, it then seems plausible to argue that something other than religion or magic can satisfy these needs in a better way. Magic does not really satisfy men's frustrated purposes, but technology might! To many of the early anthropologists religious belief was something which would give way, as men became more rational, to more realistic ways of satisfying human desires and answering human needs. The same assumption can be found in early psychoanalysis in which one can also see inheritors of Hume's legacy. There are special problems connected with their views to which we have not yet given any attention. It is to these problems that we turn in the next chapter.

NOTES

1. I owe the title of this chapter to J. B. Loudon's 'Private Stress and Public Ritual', in *Journal of Psychosomatic Research*, Vol. 10, 1966.
2. Miguel de Unamuno, 'My Religion', in *Perplexities and Paradoxes*, p. 4. I am not suggesting that this quotation represents the deeper aspects of Unamuno's work. See Alan Lacy, *Miguel de Unamuno: The Rhetoric of Existence*, Mouton Press.
3. R. R. Marett, *The Threshold of Religion*, p. xxxi.
4. 'Sociology out of its Place' (Review), in *The Human World*, No. 3, May 1971, p. 87.

Five

Freudianism and Religion

Like Marett, Freud accepted that animism as depicted by Tylor and Frazer rightly characterized the religious beliefs of primitive men. But again, like Marett, he was not content with animism as a final explanation of the character of religious belief. He too wanted to get behind the phenomenon of animism to enquire into the reasons why the primitives and others after them had peopled the world with spirits. Like Marett, he found the answer in the psychology of the individual.

> We are thus prepared to find that primitive man transposed the
> structural conditions of his own mind into the external world; and
> we may attempt to reverse the process and put back into the
> human mind what animism teaches as to the nature of things.[1]

It is for this reason that Freud is dissatisfied with Wundt's explanation of the root of taboo in terms of the fear of demons and of those objects thought to be possessed by demons. He cannot rest contented with the appeal to the demonic as a final explanation. Statements about God and the Devil must be capable of analysis in terms of statements about man.

> Neither fear nor demons can be regarded by psychology as
> 'earliest' things, impervious to any attempt at discovering their
> antecedents. It would be another matter if demons really existed.
> But we know that, like gods, they are creations of the human
> mind; they were made by something and out of something. (p. 24)

Why did Freud think it made sense to analyse religious beliefs exhaustively in terms of their non-religious antecedents? There is no single answer to this question, but, without a doubt, one aspect of a necessarily complex answer has much to do with the importance of the notion of the unconscious in Freud's work. By invoking the notion of the unconscious, Freud was able to bring out the sense in which things are not what they seem to be in people's lives, even when the people themselves are unaware of this or strenuously deny it. If religious beliefs could be shown to be a product of the unconscious, then it would follow that religious beliefs are not what they seem to be. What is meant by Freud's discovery of the unconscious is itself a vast topic which I cannot explore fully in this context. I hope to say enough, however, to raise certain difficulties about the claim that religious belief can be explained in non-religious terms as a product of the unconscious.

First, in order to consider the way, or one of the ways, in which the notion of the unconscious might enter our daily discourse, let us consider a simple but illuminating example.[2] Consider a musically gifted mother who nevertheless fails to recognize that her son's voice is nothing more than average. In the light of certain circumstances we would be prepared to say that the mother is deceiving herself. For example, every time someone points out to her the weakness in her son's voice, she has an excuse ready at hand: the performance was an exception, others were to blame, he had a cold, the music was not to his liking, and so on. Of course, all this could be true: some performances are better than others, others are to blame on occasion, singers do contract colds, performers do not relish all music to the same extent. But of this particular mother we want to conclude that the excuses have turned into an unconscious evasion of the fact that her son's voice is of poor quality. This shows in the number of excuses she has to make, her strong desire for her son's success, her dogmatic refusal to entertain a contrary view or to examine the facts, and in the fact that she is musically able and makes sound judgements where other singers are concerned. If the voice were anyone's but her son's she would have drawn an unfavourable conclusion long ago. It is the fact that she tries to avoid any counter-criticism, discussion or examination which makes us say that although she appears to be assessing her son's voice, unconsciously, she is defending him against adverse criticism and hiding from him and from herself the fact that his voice is of poor quality.

Notice in particular the way in which we discover the unconscious character of the mother's actions. We do not do so by looking for some hidden entity below the surface of events. The analogy of discovering the remainder of an iceberg when only the tip is visible is not a helpful one. It is the behaviour of the mother which leads us to our conclusions. The fact that she resists so strenuously any attempt to show her the truth is one of our main reasons for saying that she is hiding from herself the truth about her son's voice. Freud himself is not clear about the logical status of the notion of the unconscious at all times. Sometimes, he speaks of the unconscious as if it were some kind of inner force which determines men's actions, but I cannot pursue this matter further.

What I want to do in terms of our example is note some of the conditions of intelligibility which characterize our talk about the unconscious. First, in order to talk intelligibly about the unconscious we must recognize a distinction between that which is conscious and that which is unconscious. When we say that someone is unconscious of his motives or of the character of his actions, we are noting a deviation in the situation. In our example, the mother's view of why she praises her son's voice deviates from the truth. Her ways of defending her judgement deviate in important respects from what we would call defence of a judgement. The mother's description of the situation deviates from the description which ought to be given of it. As I have said, the description she offers could be true. Her son's voice could be a fine one, a performance could fail to bring this out, the son could have had a cold when someone heard him sing, and so on. These are the descriptions which the mother wants us to accept. They are perfectly natural descriptions; descriptions which have a familiar place in the lives we lead and in the society in which we live. Why, then, do we refuse to accept the mother's descriptions as satisfactory? The reason is because there is a tension between the descriptions offered and features of the situation in which they are offered, features we have already noted. When we bring this tension to the mother's notice she resists it. Because of this resistance we say that she is unconsciously defending her son.

Of course, although we say that the mother in our example is deceiving herself, she need not be described as neurotic. The points I have been stressing, however, are even clearer when applied to neurosis. Once again, in order to speak of neurotic behaviour one must imply some contrast with normality. This is not a contingent matter, but part of what we mean by the description 'neurotic'. The first condition which must be noted, then, in talking intelligibly about the unconscious in people's actions, is that there must be an implied contrast in such talk between what is conscious and what is unconscious, and, in some cases, between what is neurotic and what is normal. Psychoanalysts see their task as that of freeing people from their unconscious fears, desires, hopes, etc. by making them explicit. The emphasis on the first condition of intelligibility in our talk of the unconscious is clearly central in this context. Yet it was this very condition that Freud ignored in his discussions concerning religion.

There are two further conditions of intelligibility involved in our talk about the unconscious which are equally important. We saw that in talking of unconscious purposes etc., there was a tension between the true description of the situation and the description which the person in the grip of unconscious purposes wanted to offer of it. We want to say to such a person, 'You want us to believe that the situation is such-and-such, but, as a matter of fact, it is like this.' We offer a new description of the situation to the person who is deceiving herself or to the neurotic. But what conditions make this new description the true description of the situation? For example, I may say to someone, 'The disservice you did to that person was no accident, as you would have us believe, and as you believe yourself. The truth of the matter is that you were paying him back for being appointed to the post you wanted for yourself.' If this is to be a true description of the situation two conditions must be fulfilled. First, the description must be intelligible within the way of life which the person whom we want to so describe participates in. The importance of this condition can be illustrated as follows. What if someone suggested that what Abraham's wife really wanted, although she did not realize it, was the kind of freedom advocated today by the Women's Liberation Movement? Does the suggestion make any kind of sense? Surely not. It does not make sense because these contemporary ideas about liberation played no part in the society of Abraham's day. It is not an accident that Abraham's wife did not have such desires. It would be meaningless to attribute such desires to her, the social and cultural conditions which give such desires their meaning were not part of the kind of lives the women of her time lived. You will remember that I stressed the importance of the distinction between the conscious and the unconscious. Nevertheless, the limits of our awareness are themselves determined by the possibilities of sense and nonsense in our society and in our culture. Therefore, if a suggested description of a situation makes no sense in the social or cultural context in which the situation so described takes place, it follows that that cannot be the correct description of the situation. Again, when Freud discusses religion he ignores this second condition.

The final condition which makes it possible to offer a person a description of his actions which shows him his unconscious designs etc. is that the person himself must be capable of understanding the offered description. If a person does not understand what it means for a man to be appointed for a job that someone else wants and for that someone to resent that fact, it follows that such considerations could not be attributed to his unconscious designs. This condition is also ignored by Freud in his discussion of religion. Keeping the three conditions of the intelligibility of psychoanalysis in mind, we must now turn to a consideration of what Freud does say about religious belief.

Like Tylor, Freud too thinks that primitive rites and rituals are to be understood as an early stage in our development. Religious beliefs can be understood by reference to the neurotic people in our own society. Yet, in the light of the conditions we have just discussed, we can see that there are a host of difficulties connected with these suggestions. We saw that in order to understand neurotic behaviour we need to contrast it with some conception of normality. But Freud wants to call what is normal in the lives of peoples in different cultures from our own, a case of neurosis. In that case, how can a distinction be drawn between the normal and the neurotic? Freud's answer is to draw a distinction between primitive religion, which he regards as neurotic, and what is called normal in our society. Primitive people can be compared with our own children. But this will not do. The meaning of an individual's life is bound up with his relationships with other people, the activities he engages in, how all these hang together for him, and so on. These relationships and activities in their turn are meaningful within the context of social institutions, movements and traditions. Freud, however, wants to reverse this emphasis. He speaks as if social institutions, movements and traditions are dependent on the desires of the individual. He believes that these desires are essentially the same in all men. He is prepared to argue, furthermore, that different social practices in different cultures are analysable in terms of these fundamental desires. Freud has a static, anti-historical, view of human nature which consists of basic desires connected with human sexuality. A good example of the way in which Freud argues can be found in his comparison of two cases which he treats as though they were the same, but which, in fact, are quite different.

Here is the first case:

> A Maori chief would not blow a fire with his mouth; for his sacred breath would communicate its sanctity to the fire, which would pass it on to the pot on the fire, which would pass it on to the meat in the pot, which stood on the fire, which was breathed on by the chief; so that the eater, infected by the chief's breath conveyed through these intermediaries, would surely die.

Here is the second case:

> My patient's husband purchased a household article of some kind and brought it home with him. She insisted that it should be removed or it would make the room she lived in 'impossible'. For she had heard that the article had been bought in a shop situated in, let us say, 'Smith' Street. 'Smith', however, was the married name of a woman friend of hers who died in a distant town and whom she had known in her youth under her maiden name. This friend of hers was at the moment 'impossible' or taboo. Consequently the article that had been purchased here in Vienna was as taboo as the friend herself with whom she must not come into contact. (pp. 27–8)

Freud wants to equate the two cases. He pays no attention to the idea of the sacred which is connected with the Maori chief. The 'impossibility' of coming into contact with the sacred would be quite different in meaning from the 'impossibility' involved in one woman finding another quite impossible. Freud wants to look behind the initial account of the situation to get at the psychoanalytic account of it. This may be acceptable in terms of the second case, but what about the first case? Freud does not offer an account of the situations in terms of reasons which have their life within the activities of the tribe. Freud says that it is a waste of time to listen to the reasons of the tribesmen. Notice that he is ruling out their references to the sacred as a possible satisfactory account of their activities. Notice, in our previous examples, that the reasons offered by the people who were deceiving themselves *could* have been true. In the case of the tribesmen, however, Freud is saying that their reasons *cannot* be true because they are inherently senseless. Their reasons can be analysed in the way we analyse neurotic behaviour in our own society. Yet these assumptions ignore those very conditions of intelligibility which make psychoanalysis possible. The form of neurosis and of unconscious desires depends on the kind of society within which the neurosis occurs. But Freud wants to explain primitive religion in terms of neurosis. The point which needs to be emphasized is that social institutions, movements and traditions cannot be explained in terms of neurosis, since it is within the context of such institutions, movements and traditions that neurosis has its meaning. When Freud speaks of the whole of primitive religion as a neurosis, he is employing an unhistorical notion of neurosis which is devoid of meaning.

Freud does not take the existence of a multiplicity of social movements seriously. For Freud, culture represents demands which curtail an individual's instinctual wishes, wishes which have already taken their form and character in the first five years of his life. To ease the burden of these demands one finds narcissistic satisfaction in the achievements of one's culture. Among the culture's ideals which play this role are those of religion, that is, according to Freud, those of its illusions. One can see that man's instinctual wishes are the basic reality in terms of which cultural movements are to be understood. John Anderson points out that, for Freud, 'The individual is always the agent—or the patient of other individual agents; there is no sense of him as a 'vehicle' of social forces, as a member of movements which are just as real, just as definite as he is' and he argues, rightly, that 'unless we treat a person otherwise than as a unit, unless we consider the activities which pass *through* him (in which he participates without being *the* agent or *the* patient), we cannot even give an account of the activities which go on within him'.[3] Freud argues in exactly the opposite way, claiming that 'the principal task of civilization, its actual *raison d'être*, is to defend us against nature'.[4] Confronted with religious beliefs, Freud can therefore ask: 'What are these ideas in the light of psychology? Whence do they derive the esteem in which they are held? And, to take a further timid step, what is their real worth?' (p. 16). The answer Freud gives to this question in terms of primitive man's frustrations in the face of a demanding nature and of sustaining illusions—the wish that things might be otherwise—is too similar to the replies of Tylor, Frazer and Marett to merit repeating here. The spirit in which a solution must be sought is also similar, namely, the belief that 'scientific work is the only road which can lead us to a knowledge of reality outside ourselves' (p. 27). The result of such an enterprise is not an attitude to life which could simply merit an honourable place among others, but, rather, the only possible attitude to life, one based on a clear apprehension of reality:

> And, as for the great necessities of Fate, against which there is no help, they will learn to endure with resignation. Of what use to them is the mirage of wide acres in the moon, whose harvest no one has ever yet seen? As honest smallholders on this earth they will know how to cultivate their plot in such a way that it supports them. (p. 46)

Thus speaks the voice of a genuine inheritor of Hume's legacy.

Yet, despite the difficulties we have encountered so far, serious though they are, it might be thought that a corrective is possible which would render the relation between religion and psychoanalysis unproblematic. Let us suppose that the confusions involved in Freud's individualistic psychology were recognized; that the attempt to explain social movements in terms of a set of basic desires in the individual was abandoned. Furthermore, let us suppose that the multiplicity of social movements within the same society and as between different societies was recognized. It would then be true in practice that, as Peter Winch says,

> A psychoanalyst who wished to give an account of the aetiology of neuroses amongst, say, the Trobriand Islanders, could not just apply without further reflection the concepts developed by Freud for situations arising in our own society. He would have first to investigate such things as the idea of fatherhood among the islanders and take into account any relevant aspects in which their ideas differed from that current in his own society. And it is almost inevitable that such an investigation would lead to some modification in the psychological theory appropriate for explaining neurotic behaviour in this new situation.[5]

Extending this point, one might say that the determination of psychoanalytic treatment would also have to take into account whether religious ideas are involved in the patient's neurosis. If this is the case, due account would have to be taken of this fact. It would be impossible to do so without drawing on a distinction between normal religious practices and neurotic religious behaviour. This being the case, one could not call the normal religious practices a case of neurosis. The task of psychoanalysis, in this context, would be to free the person from his neurosis and to bring him back to normality. But that normality might well involve the holding of religious beliefs. The psychoanalyst, on this view, does not impose any scheme of significance on the patient. On the contrary, the psychoanalyst merely waits on his patient, helping him to make explicit the pattern which he, the psychoanalyst, with his greater experience, sees in the life of his patient. If we accept this account of psychoanalysis, the analyst is seen as someone who endeavours to bring out a latent meaning in a manifested muddle presented to him by his patient. Recalling our initial simple example, and applying its lesson to contexts of much greater complexity, one could say that the psychoanalyst is simply someone who helps the musically gifted mother to see that she has been unconsciously resisting the true description of the quality of her son's voice. Here, the ingredients of the situation have to do with a relationship between a mother and her son and musical criticism. But if the ingredients had consisted of religious ideas and relationships, the task of psychoanalysis would be the same. It would not be the task of psychoanalysis to explain away these ideas.

The picture offered of psychoanalysis is an attractive one, but I do not think it can be accepted as a complete picture. Accepting it obscures too many aspects of Freud's conception of psychoanalysis, and, I believe, of contemporary psychoanalysis. I cannot pursue this latter point, but certain matters of relevance will emerge in a further consideration of Freud's work. What is underestimated in the above account is the fact that for Freud, not *any* resting point would do as a final explanation. For him, all psychoanalytic explanations lead back to themes which have a sexual character, or which relate to the destructive tendencies of the death instinct. The insistence on such an emphasis brings out problems connected with the relationship between psychoanalysis and religion that we have yet to consider.

The problems I have in mind can be brought out by a consideration of further examples. In the example we have already considered, the move from a state of self-deception to a recognition of how things are is a move from the familiar to the familiar. What I mean by this is that the example of the musically gifted mother is one which contains both in the self-deception involved and the description of the true state of affairs, features of our lives which are perfectly familiar to us. We can say of the mother that she came to see how things were where the quality of her son's voice was concerned and her own attempts to resist facing the truth. The picture of psycho-analysis we have been offered is one in which it is seen as a method of bringing people to see how things are in their lives. I am not arguing that this view of psychoanalysis is entirely confused, but simply that, in certain contexts, it begins to exhibit strains and tensions.

To illustrate this argument, let us consider a further example. A woman, having been given generous leave by her employer, begins to develop violent headaches.[6] The example does not strike us as so familiar as the previous example. Good fortune is not normally followed by violent headaches. If such headaches occur they might be put down to bad luck. Why should there be thought to be any connection? As a result of analysis, however, it emerges that the woman's strong sense of independence felt threatened by her em-ployer's generosity. Furthermore, the strong sense of independence is shown to be a reaction to an unconscious need for dependence. Something called out for an explanation and the woman comes to this as an account of how things are in her life. Yet, the acceptance of this account does not depend on remembering certain events, as it might do in our previous example: moments of evasion, dogmatic assertions, half-recognitions, and so on. Rather, the acceptance is the product of a reflection on the course her life has taken which concludes that these emphases, forming this pattern of interpretation, makes better sense of her life than any other. In the second example, this is what we would *mean* by coming to see things as they are.

Consider a third example taken from Freud himself. He tells us of a woman who, obsessively, ran into a room in her house, straightened the tablecloth, rang for her maid, and then sent the maid away again on some trivial errand. Under analysis she recalled that there was a stain on the tablecloth and that she adjusted the cloth in such a way that the maid would be bound to see the stain. Freud explains that

The whole scene proved to be the reproduction of an incident in her marriage. On the wedding-night her husband had met with a not unusual mishap. He found himself impotent, and 'many times in the course of the night came hurrying from his room to hers' in order to try again. In the morning he said he would be shamed in the eyes of the hotel chambermaid who made the bed, so he took a bottle of red ink and poured its contents over the sheet; but he did it so clumsily that the stain came in a place most unsuitable for his purpose. With her obsessive act, therefore, she was reproducing the bridal night.[7]

This example is very different from the previous two. The example does not begin with something familiar to us, but with a strange obsessive action. No amount of reflection on her behaviour would bring us to Freud's explanation. What clinches the matter are the events which took place on the bridal night. Yet, precisely because the explanation depends on historical evidence, the evidence by its very nature is falsifiable.

Now let us consider a fourth example which, at first, seems very close to the third. Freud, in his analyses, often claims to be explaining the meaning of people's neuroses in terms of traumatic sexual experiences which took place during their childhood: witnessing their parents having intercourse, wanting to kill one's father because he is seen as a sexual competitor for one's mother's favours, being threatened with castration, and so on. It is natural to think that Freud is appealing to historical events in the same sense as the events of the bridal night in our previous example. At one time, he certainly seemed to think that he was. He had to admit, however, that it was quite clear from many of his cases that these events had not actually occurred in the childhood of the patient. Yet, in admitting this it was also clear that the absence of historical confirmation and even the proven absence of the alleged event, did not mean that Freud thought his analyses worthless:

> I should myself be glad to know whether the primal scene in my present patient's case was a phantasy or a real experience; but, taking other similar cases into account, I must admit that the answer to this question is not in reality a matter of very great importance. These scenes of obsessing parental intercourse, of being seduced in childhood, and of being threatened with castration are unquestionably an inherited endowment, a phylogenetic inheritance, but they may just as easily be acquired by personal experience . . . All that we find in the prehistory of

neuroses is that a child catches hold of this phylogenetic experience where his own experience fails him. He fills in the gaps in individual truth with prehistoric truth; he replaces occurrences in his own life by occurrences in the life of his ancestors.[8]

Where the childhood traumatic sexual events have not occurred in a person's childhood, such events have been the content of the fantasies of every child. In this way, Freud's thesis about the determining role of infantile sexuality becomes unfalsifiable. Take, for instance, the generality Freud ascribes to the phenomenon he called the Oedipus complex. Freud claimed that if the tensions associated with it were not resolved in childhood, they would show later in adult life. But what if no tensions do show in adult life? Freud would have to claim that they have been resolved in the course of natural development. He has to make this claim because he claims that these tensions *must* be part of the unconscious experience of every child. This being so he could not appeal to the adults who experienced no tensions later in life to remember these tensions during their childhood, since the tensions were unconscious. The only other verification would be from parents or other people noting features of the child's behaviour which would make the ascription of such tensions appropriate. Yet, even in the absence of such evidence Freud would say that this phenomenon *must* be part of every child's unconscious experience. This shows that the 'must', the necessity, is not based on biographical evidence.

The language of sexuality, in Freud's development of it, becomes quite technical. Within the appeal to the sexual one could have explanations offered in terms of the Oedipus complex, castration complex, penis envy, etc., etc. The variety of explanations blurred the fact that the limits of possible explanations were always within the realm of the sexual. Compared with our previous examples, we seem to have come a long way. We began with familiar cases of self-deception being explained in familiar terms, but end with the familiar, jokes, slips of the tongue, legends, morality, religion, being explained in terms of unfamiliar language concerning sexuality.

How is the appeal to the sexual in Freud to be understood as a form of explanation? The first thing to be clear about is that at times such an appeal clearly did provide the correct explanation. The same can be said of Freud's thesis that our dreams are the products of unfulfilled sexual wishes. The same again can be said of Freud's

F

thesis that adult neuroses must be explained in terms of childhood events. All these theses are true on particular occasions. But this would not be enough for Freud. Wittgenstein says that Freud

> ... wanted to find some one explanation which would show what dreaming is. He wanted to find the *essence* of dreaming. And he would have rejected any suggestion that he might be partly right but not altogether so. If he was partly wrong, that would have meant for him that he was wrong altogether—that he had not really found the essence of dreaming.[9]

Yet, even if we admit the *a priori* element in the appeal to the sexual in Freud, how is this appeal to be understood, and what bearing does it have on Freud's discussions of religion?

Wittgenstein points out that if sex is a preoccupation for someone, then he may account for the significance of most things in his life in relation to it. This is what happens with Freud's analysis of dreams: 'no matter what you start from, the association will lead finally and inevitably back to that same theme. Freud remarks on how, after an analysis of it, the dream appears so very logical. And of course it does' (p. 51). The inevitability of the course of the association has led many to argue as follows:

> Freud had the original and suggestive idea that dreams were really wish fulfilments, and not only that but always sexual wish fulfilments. Some dreams obviously are. But others on the face of it were not. So in order to save his beloved hypothesis he had to invent a great many subsidiary hypotheses, those that he described under the name of the dream mechanisms: condensation, displacement of affect, symbolism, etc., etc. He does not seem to have observed that in so introducing all these extra hypotheses he has emasculated his original idea of all significance. Let me make this clearer by an incident which Janet relates. Janet was talking to an enthusiastic pupil of Freud: 'Last night,' said Janet, 'I dreamt that I was standing on a railway station: surely that has no sexual significance.' 'Oh! indeed it has,' said the Freudian; 'a railway station is a place where trains go to and fro, to and fro, and all to and fro movements are highly suggestive. And what about a railway signal; it can be either up or down, need I say more?' Now as Janet rightly went on to point out, if you allow

yourself such a freedom in symbolism, every possible content of your dream whatsoever can be forced into this type of interpretation. The theory has become 'fact proof'; it just can't be refuted. But that which cannot be proved wrong by any conceivable experience is without meaning. (Drury, pp. 16–17)

I agree that it has been shown that Freud is not offering an hypothesis or an explanation. But it does not follow from this that his appeal to the sexual is without meaning. Its meaning may be other than that which resides in an hypothesis or an explanation. Wittgenstein suggests, I believe rightly, that the meaning of the appeal does lie elsewhere. First, one must note the obvious, namely, that Freud appealed to something which is a force and which is important in people's lives. Furthermore, the kind of appeal he makes is exciting to many people. In a letter to Norman Malcolm, Wittgenstein says of Freud:

He always stresses what great forces in the mind, what strong prejudices work against the idea of psycho-analysis. But he never says what an enormous charm the idea has for people, just as it has for Freud himself. There may be strong prejudices against uncovering something nasty, but sometimes it is infinitely more *attractive* than it is repulsive.[10]

On rare occasions, Freud himself admits this. In a letter to a friend he writes, 'The sexual business attracts people; they all go away impressed and convinced, after exclaiming: No one has ever asked me that before.'[11] People are prepared to bring various incidents in their own lives into relation with the sexual. Drury is quite right to deny that this always has the force of an explanation or hypothesis. But why can't we say that what we have here is things being looked at from the aspect of the sexual? By looking at things in this way, their aspect changes too. Wittgenstein makes this point in relation to dreams:

In considering what a dream is, it is important to consider what happens to it, the way its aspect changes when it is brought into relation with other things remembered, for instance. On first awaking a dream may impress one in various ways. One may be terrified and anxious; or when one has written the dream down one may have a certain sort of thrill, feel a very lively interest in it, feel intrigued by it. If one now remembers certain events in the previous day and connects what was dreamed with these, this already makes a difference, changes the aspect of the dream. If reflecting on the dream then leads one to remember certain things in early childhood, this will give it a different aspect still. And so on. (All this is connected with what was said about dreaming the dream over again. It still belongs to the dream, in a way.) (p. 46)

In such associations, what one has is not an explanation of the dream, but forms of reflection on the dream. When these reflections are sexual in character, they show you something about the person who reflects in this way. The fact that he is prepared to associate certain things with the sexual shows something about him. Also, one may come to see something about oneself through the patterns one's associations take. Wittgenstein introduces the necessary distinction one has to make when he says, 'One may be able to discover certain things about oneself by this sort of free association, but it does not explain why the dream occurred' (p. 51). Nevertheless, because the limits of Freud's analyses do not have the status of explanations or hypotheses it does not follow that they do not have a bearing on people's lives, since the analyses changed the aspect of incidents in those lives which trouble people in one way or another. Furthermore, it must be remembered that the practice of psycho-analysis itself has an influence on people's lives and on the society in which it is carried on. It itself is one factor in accounting for the increased emphasis which people may give to sexual matters. Freud's genius consisted in the analyses that he offered in this context. Cioffi says that

Freud certainly produced statements to which an enormous number of people have said 'yes', but there are good grounds for assimilating his achievements to that of the anonymous geniuses to whom it first occurred that Tuesday is lean and Wednesday fat, the low notes on the piano dark and the high notes light. Except that instead of words, notes and shades, we have scenes from human life.

Cioffi says that it is impossible to explain our interest in Freud, and the influence he has had on us, 'without invoking what Wittgenstein called "charm". We were caused to re-dream our life in surroundings such that its apsect changed—and it was the charm that made us do it' (pp. 209–10).

What are the consequences of these conclusions for Freud's discussion of religion? Here, too, we have the claim that he has explained the genesis of religious belief, such that once one has grasped and accepted the explanation, religious beliefs, like neuroses, need exercise a hold on us no longer. But we may find that, as in previous contexts, what Freud has done is to offer an aspect on life, a way of looking at things, which changes the significance of religion for those who accept it. One example will be sufficient to illustrate this.

Freud thought his analyses of religious belief were relevant, not simply to primitive religion, but to any form of religion. He put forward the somewhat alarming thesis that religion has its origins in common complicity in a murder. Freud suggested that patriarchal hordes had broken up as the result of the murder of the father by the sons who envied his sexual prerogatives. The reasons for killing the father are found in the Oedipus complex, in the father being envied because he is seen as a sexual competitor for the favours of the female. But once they had killed the father, the sons regretted it. The dead father becomes more influential in their lives than the living one had been. They now want to appease his spirit for the wrong they have done, and this, according to Freud, is the explanation of the sacrifices which were made to the totem animal. On the other hand, the attitude of the sons to the dead father is an essentially ambivalent one. Though they love him, they also hate him at the same time. Therefore, although sacrifices are made to the totem animal (which is really a symbol for the father), one finds that at special times the killing of the totem animal is allowed. They re-enact the original murder. Freud traces the principle of emotional ambivalence in various historical contexts, for example, in the notion of the divinity of kings. Finally, he analyses the eating of bread and the drinking of wine in the Christian holy communion. According to Freud, an attempt has been made to lessen the guilt for killing the father—the Father himself now provides the sacrifice. Nevertheless, in eating flesh and drinking blood the original murder is repeated yet again. That is why Freud can close *Totem and Taboo* with the words, 'In the beginning was the Deed'.

What are we to make of all this? If one takes Freud's analysis as an explanation which depends on historical confirmation, it is completely without foundation. If one takes the analysis to indicate the origins of the idea of God as a Father, it does not take us very far. We soon run into the confusion we have already come across which results from failing to distinguish between the meaning of an idea and the way it originated. It is one thing to say that God would not be called 'Father' unless men possessed the notion of an earthly father, but quite another thing to conclude from this that whatever one says about a heavenly father can be explained in terms of what we can say about earthly fathers. Yet, even if we accept these conclusions, we have seen that one aspect of Freud's analysis remains unaffected by them. Freud need not be taken as offering us either an explanation of religious belief or an account of its meaning. Rather, what he is offering is a competing way of looking at things, a rival set of emphases, such that, if they are adopted, religious belief no longer claims the allegiance of the people concerned. Wittgenstein expresses the point as follows:

> Freud refers to various ancient myths in these connexions, and claims that his researches have now explained how it came about that anybody should think or propound a myth of that sort.
>
> Whereas in fact Freud has done something different. He has not given a scientific explanation of the ancient myth. What he has done is to propound a new myth. The attractiveness of the suggestion, for instance, that all anxiety is a repetition of the anxiety of the birth trauma, is just the attractiveness of a mythology. 'It is all the outcome of something that happened long ago.' Almost like referring to a totem. (pp. 50–1)

What general conclusions can be drawn from the discussions in this chapter about the relations between religious belief and psychoanalysis? First, we have seen that, in certain contexts, psychoanalysts can be seen as simply waiting on the accounts of their troubles given by their patients. Their activities can be seen as bringing the patient to see how things are in his life. If the troubles of the patient involve religious ideas, the analyst may well have to take account of distinctions between normality and abnormality in religion in order to determine whether his patient is neurotic or not.[12] This being so, psychoanalysis could hardly be seen as an attempt to explain away religious ideas. Second, we have seen that psychoanalysis, in certain contexts, seems to offer a distinctive way of looking at incidents in one's life. This way of looking at things, in which an appeal to the sexual plays a prominent part, militates against the emphasis found in religious belief. Instead of 'In the beginning was the Word' we are offered, 'In the beginning was the Deed'. It is not that the latter explains the former or shows it to be mistaken, but that if one gives one's allegiance to the latter it is difficult to see how one can give one's allegiance to the former also.

Before we leave the topic of Freudianism and Religion, it is important to remember that Freud *himself* did think that he was offering an explanation of religious belief. Because of this he made certain claims, in relation to religion, which it is important to recognize as confusions. There are three of these I want to note. The first we have already discussed, namely, Freud's belief that religious belief could be called a neurosis and treated accordingly. The second confusion in fact stems from the first confusion. Because Freud believed that religious beliefs were forms of neurosis, the explanations he offered of them set unnecessary limits on what could be of importance to human beings. The limits of acceptability set by his explanations blinded Freud to certain possibilities of meaning expressed in various religious beliefs and practices. This is brought out by the way in which Freud thought that such beliefs and practices could be explained in terms of emotional ambivalence. Consider Freud's treatment of taboos concerning the treatment of enemies and taboos relating to the dead.

Freud tells us that although we should expect primitive peoples to be cruel to their enemies (why Freud should think this is unclear) we do not find this confirmed by the facts.

> We shall be greatly interested to learn, then, that even in their case the killing of a man is governed by a number of observances which are included among the usages of taboo. These observances fall easily into four groups. They demand (1) the appeasement of the slain enemy, (2) restrictions upon the slayer, (3) acts of expiation and purification by him and (4) certain ceremonial observances.[13]

Freud gives the following examples of rites of appeasement from Frazer. The first concerns warriors returning home in triumph to the island of Timor:

On the occasion of the expedition's return, sacrifices are offered
to appease the souls of the men whose heads have been taken. 'The
people think that some misfortune would befall the victor were
such offerings omitted.' Moreover, a part of the ceremony consists
of a dance accompanied by a song, in which the death of the slain
man is lamented and his forgiveness is entreated. 'Be not angry,'
they say, 'because your head is here with us; had we been less
lucky, our heads might now have been exposed in your village.
We have offered the sacrifice to appease you. Your spirit may now
rest and leave us in peace. Why were you our enemy? Would it
not have been better that we should remain friends? Then your
blood would not have been spilt and your head would not have
been cut off.' (p. 37)

The second example is as follows:

Other peoples have found a means of changing their former
enemies after their death into guardians, friends and benefactors.
This method lies in treating their severed heads with affection, as
some of the savage races of Borneo boast of doing. When the Sea
Dyaks of Sarawak bring home a head from a successful
head-hunting expedition, for months after its arrival it is treated
with the greatest consideration and addressed with all the names
of endearment of which their language is capable. The most dainty
morsels of food are thrust into its mouth, delicacies of all kinds and
even cigars. The head is repeatedly implored to hate its former
friends and to love its new hosts since it has now become one of
them. (p. 37)

Freud refuses to explain these practices in terms of superstition.
For him, they are rooted in emotional ambivalence, a mixture of
hatred, admiration, remorse, happiness at having killed, and a bad
conscience in relation to the dead. The rituals are ways of coming to
terms with this ambivalence. The first, a way of appeasing the dead,
and the second, a way of changing the dead into benefactors. But
why should we accept this account? Whether certain activities show
that kind of ambivalence Freud is talking about depends on our
being able to judge these activities with others, similar in character,
where such ambivalence is absent. What the facts are where the
tribes Freud mentions are concerned could not be answered without

knowledge of them. Yet, possibilities other than those Freud mentions come readily to mind, possibilities which are ruled out *a priori* by Freud's psychoanalytic assumptions. The issue is not to determine which possibility is the correct one, but the recognition of alternative accounts as possibilities.

Consider the following example. In a film called *Zulu* an incident is depicted which happened in the Zulu War at the battle of Rorke's Drift. Despite many charges inflicting heavy losses on the British garrison, the Zulus realize that they cannot overrun it. The soldiers in the garrison see the hills lined once again with Zulu warriors and expect another attack. Instead, the Zulus raise their weapons in salute and depart. Here is a gesture, a tribute, which transcends the distinction between friend and foe. It has nothing to do with emotional ambivalence towards the enemy. On the contrary, this tribute to bravery and valour has its meaning from within a tradition of warrior values.[14] A given warrior's attitude to these values might be ambivalent, but one cannot analyse the values themselves in these terms. Could not the same be said of the examples Freud offers us concerning the treatment of slain prisoners? In these practices the dead are honoured in various ways. The songs and dances in their honour transcend the differences between the victor and the vanquished, the slayer and the slain. But to say this is not to explain these practices or to postulate some emotional need which they serve. This is what the practices express. The first example may involve appeasement and a belief that misfortune follows failure to seek it. But what such appeasement and misfortune amount to may be internally related to what is involved in dishonouring the dead. The second example may not be an attempt to manipulate the dead in any pragmatic way, but the expression of honour in the form of an act of adoption.

Freud is blind to these possibilities. For him, the rituals must be something other than they seem to be. When they are explained they can be seen as attempts to come to terms with emotional ambivalence. He does not see the rituals as the expressions of certain values and attitudes which are not *for* anything, but which constitute ways of regarding battle, defeat, victory, the slayer and the slain. Freud could have avoided these confusions if he had taken more seriously an objection he once put to himself:

But after all taboo is not a neurosis but a social institution. We are therefore faced with the task of explaining what difference there is in principle between a neurosis and a cultural creation such as taboo.[15]

Freud never did take this task seriously. Had he done so, he would have seen that he was using one way of emphasizing incidents in human life, a way deeply rooted in his own culture, as a yardstick with which to explain practices in other cultures. In this way, his own understanding of the variety in the lives men lead is severely limited. Just as he wanted to find the essence of dreaming, so Freud wanted to study man as man. Inevitably, since there is no such creature as universal man, such an enterprise must lead to distortion and conceptual confusion. Freud's confusion in his treatment of taboos concerning prisoners of war is, in this respect, similar to Blanshard's treatment of the same question, by which he tries to determine, once and for all, as it were, how a rational man should behave in such circumstances.

Blanshard says that

> Modern man would claim some advance over ancient Assyria in respect to the treatment of prisoners of war. Suppose that he could catch an ancient Assyrian by the beard and expostulate with him about the practice of torturing prisoners of war for his own pleasure. Could he offer any relevant *arguments* to show that the Assyrian practice was wrong? He would have no doubt he could. He could say that to act in this way was to produce gratuitous pain or at least pain that was far greater than any pleasure it produced; and that this was wrong; he could show that it was to indulge one's impulses to hatred and to satisfaction in others' misery, and that this was wrong too. If then he was asked why these should be called wrong, could he continue the argument? He could say that to produce intense pain was wrong because such pain was evil. If he were asked to give reasons for these judgements again, he would probably be nonplussed. He has arrived here at judgements that he would be content to regard as self-evident. But at any rate he has offered an ethical argument.[16]

In a critical review, A. E. Murphy comments,

> And surely it is one of the strangest arguments on record. I know little about the reasoning processes of the ancient Assyrian, but

recalling that he came down like a wolf on the fold I should question this as a prudent approach to even the most ancient of the breed.[17]

Murphy's criticisms of Blanshard are similar to the criticisms we have made of Freud:

> Suppose that Blanshard and his friend, the 'modern' man, had really been concerned to reach an understanding with the Assyrian on the wrong of treating prisoners, and not simply to argue with complete rational cogency from premises which were to them self-evident: is it thus that they would proceed? Of course not. A 'common' argument requires common grounds or reasons, and so far none have been supplied that bear, save truistically, on the case at issue . . . the Assyrian's notion of what it is proper to do with prisoners is bound up, as it is bound to be, with the form of life of which the glorification of war and warriors and 'the right way' of treating enemies are a part. (p. 239)

Blanshard describes the Assyrian as torturing the prisoners for his own pleasure. Freud says that taboos concerning prisoners are means of coming to terms with emotional ambivalence. Yet the torture may not be *for* anything. Murphy advances one suggestion regarding what it may express:

> . . . if the torture of prisoners glorifies the state and its gods and celebrates the triumph of the superior race over its enemies, it has served its purpose in a worthy cause. We need not go to Assyria for that kind of argument: there was plenty of it in Japan during the second World War, and some much nearer home. (p. 238)

But there are other possibilities. A warrior, in being captured, may be humiliated and shamed. He is deprived of the opportunity to win honour and glory. In captivity pain is inflicted on him. But the pain inflicted is a way of honouring the captive, not of torturing him. An opportunity is given to a warrior to show bravery in bearing pain, an opportunity to do so in battle having been taken away from him by his capture. How to treat prisoners of war, or what such treatment consists in, is not something which can be determined in abstraction by a study of man as man. Freud and Blanshard are guilty of the same confusion: instead of explaining emotional ambivalence and ways of obtaining pleasure in terms of human activities, where such aims have meaning, they attempt to explain human activities and social institutions in terms of such aims.

Having considered Freud's treatment of taboos concerning the treatment of prisoners at some length, his discussion of taboos concerning the dead can be noted briefly. For Freud, these taboos are rooted in fear of the dead. The dead are feared because of the emotional ambivalence which characterized relationships with the dead persons when they were alive. This ambivalence in turn was related to the sexual in ways we have already discussed. The essence of Freud's view is also expressed by Schopenhauer: 'For all love, however ethereally it may bear itself, is rooted in the sexual impulse alone, nay it absolutely is only a more definitely determined, specialised, and indeed in the strictest sense individualised sexual impulse.'[18] But why must sexual love be the most fundamental kind of love, the kind which explains all other kinds of love? Sexual love is only one kind of love, and there are others from which people can learn. Why *must* relationships with the dead be connected with the sexual? Why can't they be connected with honour, respect, continuity, ethical values, etc., etc.? Why *must* such connections be ruled out? Why *must* they be explicable in terms of the sexual? What sort of a 'must' is being employed here?

No doubt there are examples of the dead being feared, but, according to Cassirer,

> In most cases ... the opposite tendency prevails. With all their powers the survivors strain to detain the spirit in their neighbourhood. Very often the corpse is buried in the house itself where it maintains its permanent dwelling place. The ghosts of the deceased become household gods; and the life and prosperity of the family depend on their assistance and favour. At his death the parent is implored not to go away. 'We ever loved and cherished you', says a song quoted by Tylor, 'and have lived long together under the same roof; Desert it not now! Come to your home! It is swept for you, and clean; and we are there who loved you ever; and there is rice put for you; and water; Come home, come home, come to us again.'[19]

No doubt some contemporary philosophers will want to ask. 'And *did* the departed one come home?' but that question shows that the superstitious ones are not the people who sang that song, but the philosophers who ask that question. As I have said elsewhere, as long as a people can sing that song they are one with the dead, the song expresses that unity.[20] But it is a unity of respect and love; it is not sexual in character. In his treatment of taboos concerning the dead and taboos concerning the treatment of prisoners, the emphases contained in Freud's psychoanalytic explanations set limits on what is acceptable as an ultimate account of human activities and so blind Freud to other possibilities. This, together with Freud's attempt to characterize religious belief as a neurosis, are two of the three confusions involved in Freud's discussion of religious belief which I referred to earlier. The third confusion is closely connected with the other two. Throughout the discussion so far we have seen that Freud like Marett, wanted to get behind religious beliefs to the emotional ambivalence and sexual motivation which, he claimed, explained them. The third confusion is the way in which Freud's individualistic psychology wrecks any possibility of his giving serious attention to the heterogeneity of social movements, and leads to a falsification of personal and social facts. The character of this confusion has been powerfully exposed by John Anderson.

Men do not simply have one aim, happiness, to which everything else is subordinated. In his obituary article on Freud, Ernest Jones had said:

Even pure 'unhappiness' is now a medico-psychological problem. As a result of all this innumerable people now consult physicians who used either to suffer their troubles as best they could or to seek some form of consolation. I should be surprised to hear that Oscar Wilde ever sought medical advice for his mental condition, still less Dr. Johnson, Schopenhauer or Dean Swift; nor does Herr Hitler. Yet these, and thousands of others, would probably have had a happier life had they done so.[21]

Anderson comments,

Can anyone seriously doubt that Hitler would not have *wanted* to lead a happier life, to engage in the activities which a physician might have shown him had been thwarted in his earlier days, that he would consider the activities in which he is now engaged to be vastly more important? And is it not at least arguable that a man

who 'suffers his troubles as best he can' will be a better worker in
a movement than one who runs to a doctor to get relief? More
generally, can 'heroic values', can heroism and devotion, be
reduced to, or at all accounted for in terms of, the pursuit of
happiness? The 'medico-psychological' approach prevents the
Freudians from getting more than a glimpse of these problems,
and involves them ('unconsciously' no doubt) in the use of a scale
of importance which falsifies the social facts. (p. 342)

The first point to note, then, is that there are values of various kinds
which cannot be reduced to a single notion of happiness. The second
point to note is that if there are autonomous values inherent in
various social movements and institutions, they cannot be accounted
for as rationalizations; as sublimations of instinctual wishes which
have been transformed to a sphere where they cannot be harmed. All
sorts of pressures may interfere with a man's work as a scientist or
as an artist, but this does not mean that science and art can be
explained as escape roots from the frustrations caused by such
pressures:

> For one thing the materials on which scientist and artist work are
> as 'outer' as anything can be; but so, likewise, are their 'workings'
> —thinking and creating (more exactly, what thinks and what
> creates) exist in exactly the same sense (and in the same 'world')
> as the things they deal with, and do not have a bogey existence
> which falls short of 'reality'. (p. 343)

Freud fails to recognize this and as a result his account of science
and art impoverishes these activities. This can be illustrated by an
example from another context, that of sport. If my support of a
football team is to be explained in terms of narcissistic satisfaction,
in a transfer of my thwarted instincts which find fulfilment in 'my
team', the notion of genuine support for a team is impoverished.
Supporting the efforts of others is always, ultimately, a fulfilment
of my own desires.

Thirdly, because of Freud's postulation of fundamental drives and
desires which underlie what he calls civilization, he cannot account
for any genuine development in or interaction between social movements. Anderson points out that although energy can be transferred
from one activity to another, there is no ground for saying that the

energy is always sexual in character. One could argue that the energy exemplified in common work is just as original. Furthermore, if Freud is serious in his talk of the transference of sexual energy, he must recognize the reality of the non-sexual. Thus, in our example in the last chapter concerning St. Theresa's description of her vision of an angel, if we are to talk of the transformation of the sexual, we must recognize the reality of a religion in which such transformation can take place. But once such realities are recognized it no longer becomes feasible to explain them in terms of an initial set of tendencies in the individual.

> Thus, recognising the multiplicity of forms of activity in any man in any society, however primitive, we have no need to attempt the derivation of beauty from 'the realms of sexual sensation'; and we can see immediately the falsity of the assertion (p. 36 of *Civilization and its Discontents*) that 'the love of beauty is a perfect example of a feeling with an inhibited aim'. For love of beauty is concerned with things just as definite, and brings about just as definite results, as sexuality does. (p. 344)

Since science, art, morality, religion, etc. are just as definite as sexuality, they cannot be explained in terms of the latter. For the same reason they cannot be explained in terms of early sexual events in childhood. The backward glance to childhood may not simply be unnecessary, but, at times, clearly unintelligible. As Anderson points out, to explain why X has become Y there is no necessity to suppose that Y is somehow latent in X. There is another obvious possibility, namely, that the development has come about through C which is an activity which naturally occurs in adult life. It occurs then because the conditions for its development are not in the child.

> Thus it is a plain fact of human history that many types of activity do not arise at all until later life, and to say that their potentiality, their basis, that out of which they come, must have been present in infancy is really to deny interaction. (p. 353)

In the course of this chapter we have discussed the possibility of regarding Freud's psychoanalytic accounts as offering people a myth-ology, an aspect under which to view incidents in their lives. On this view, psychoanalysis could not show that religious beliefs are mistaken. It simply offers a different kind of salvation. We have also considered the possibility that psychoanalysts simply help people to see how things are in their lives, without passing judgement on the values adhered to by their patients. Here, too, there is no question of psychoanalysis showing religious belief to be a product of emotional instability. These two views of psychoanalysis cannot be reconciled either in theory or in practice, but what is ragged must be left ragged. On the other hand, it is clear that Freud himself would not be content with either view of his discussion of religious belief. Clearly, he saw himself as offering explanations of religious belief, explanations which, once recognized, free men from the illusion of religion. In thinking this Freud was confused. We have noted three fundamental confusions involved in his arguments. First, religion as such cannot be classified as a neurosis. Second, Freud's explanations set limits on what is possible in human life and blind him to other possibilities. Third, these other possibilities are present in a multiplicity of social movements, movements to which, because of his individualistic psychology, Freud could not pay serious attention.

Freud could not see that common work and common interest are often sufficient in themselves to account for human beings being engaged together in common enterprises. Like Hobbes, Freud had to ask why human beings *should* engage in common activities, and like his illustrious predecessor, he too gave an answer in terms of individual advantage. Freud tried to smuggle the social into his theory in his talk of the individual internalizing cultural demands, but it does not conceal the deficiencies in his theory.

Anderson points out that there is no objection to talking of common activities characterizing various stages of an individual's development. Neither is there any objection to talking of the influence of the earlier stages on the later stages in that development. This is no more than one would expect.

'But', as Anderson says, 'it is a far cry from this to the description of work, war and religion . . . as "products of infantile neurosis", to the contention . . . that the extreme helplessness of long duration of man's infancy are "ultimately responsible for his neurotic anxiety and his animism—or habit of projecting his own infantile feelings upon his environment—and that his animism, in particular his tendency to rediscover the good and bad parents of his unconscious fantasy in the persons of his leaders and his enemies, is responsible both for his co-operative and competitive tendencies, for his social solidarity, and for his proneness to war". These extraordinary claims would imply that infants make society; actually, they are born into society, into a set of interrelated social movements or institutions, which largely determine their history —and, by being brought into new movements, the adult can develop activities of which no trace could be found in the infant.' (pp. 353–4)

In the last three chapters we have been concerned with various attempts to provide psychological explanations of religious beliefs. We have seen that much of the trouble in these explanations comes from 'the view that individuals form society instead of society forming individuals' (p. 350). Yet, when social factors *are* emphasized in accounts of religious belief, does it mean that such accounts are free from confusion? Or shall we find in sociological, as well in psychological, accounts of religion the inheritors of Hume's philosophical legacy?

NOTES

1. Freud, *Totem and Taboo*, p. 91.
2. I owe this example to my colleague, Mr. H. O. Mounce, who uses it in his paper 'Self-Deception', in *Proceedings Aristotelian Society*, Supp. Vol. XLV, 1971, to which I am generally indebted on this topic.
3. John Anderson, 'Freudianism and Society', in *Studies in Empirical Philosophy*, p. 341.
4. Freud, *The Future of an Illusion*, p. 11.
5. Peter Winch, *The Idea of a Social Science*, p. 90.
6. This example is taken from Herbert Fingarette, *The Self in Transformation*, p. 28.
7. Freud, *Collected Papers*, Vol. II, p. 29.
8. Freud, *Collected Papers*, Vol. III, pp. 577–8.
9. Wittgenstein, *Lectures and Conversations on Aesthetics, Psychology and Religious Belief*, pp. 47–8.
10. Norman Malcolm, *Memoir of Wittgenstein*, pp. 44–5.
11. Freud, *Origins of Psychoanalysis*, Letter 14, quoted by Frank Cioffi, 'Wittgenstein's Freud', in *Studies in the Philosophy of Wittgenstein*, edited by Peter Winch. I am indebted to much in Cioffi's paper in this chapter.
12. I am not suggesting that the distinction between normality or abnormality in religion or elsewhere is a sharp one. See Drury, 'Madness and Religion', op. cit.

G

13. Freud, *The Future of an Illusion*, p. 36.
14. This is not to say that the values were always observed then, any more than they are now.
15. *Totem and Taboo*, p. 71.
16. Brand Blanshard, *Reason and Goodness*, p. 229.
17. A. E. Murphy, 'Blanshard on Good in General', in *Philosophical Review*, Vol. 72, 1963, p. 238.
18. Schopenhauer, 'Metaphysics of the Love of the Sexes', in *The World As Will and Idea*, p. 339.
19. Ernst Cassirer, *The Myth of the State*, p. 87.
20. See *Death and Immortality*, Ch. 4.
21. Ernest Jones. Obituary Article on Freud, in *International Journal of Psycho-analysis*, Vol. XXI, Pt. 1, p. 16.

Six

Religion as a Social Product

So far, in discussing the accounts of religion offered by Frazer, Tylor, Marett and Freud, what we have found is that, despite important differences, they have all been concerned with a conscious reduction-ism in their treatment of religious belief. At some stage or other they all attribute an error to the worshipper, the error of animism. Either because of his intellectual primitiveness, his emotional instability, or his unconscious desires, man projects into the outer world features of his own character. This notion of projection they owe to Ludwig Feuerbach. That Feuerbach was an inheritor of Hume's philosophical legacy has been shown by Eugene Kamenka:

> He does not confront religion as an external critic, as one who is simply concerned to show that there is no God. This, Freuerbach believed, was work successfully completed by the eighteenth-century Enlightenment. The point now was to understand religion, to show its genesis in something non-supernatural in terms of which it could be explained and understood, thus undermining the supernatural pretensions of religion at the same time as accounting for them. Feuerbach's method, applied and extended by such thinkers as Marx and Freud has become one of the standard ways of dealing with 'ideologies' as opposed to theories—we show how they arose and what needs they satisfy or what language they appeal to.[1]

What Feuerbach said about projection is, by now, a familiar story to us in this essay. A tension is created between man's wishes and his achievements. Religious beliefs are expressions of wishes; fantasies and dreams which convince a man that his thwarted desires have been fulfilled. As man gains control over areas of human life, so religion loses its hold on him. Man worships his own ideals in objectifying the notions of knowledge, will and love. Yet, one can never move from such ideals to the notion of the supernatural. One cannot do so by describing the attributes ascribed to God as infinite: infinite knowledge, infinite love, etc., etc. Feuerbach argues that

> The mystery of the inexhaustible fulness of the divine predicates is . . . nothing else than the mystery of human nature considered as an infinitely varied, infinitely modifiable, but consequently, phenomenal being.[2]

Kamenka, commenting on this remark, says:

> Infinity is not a property to be distinguished from the finite, it is merely an extension of the finite in numerical terms, it is an endless addition of more finite properties or events, it does not rise above finitude but merely keeps extending it in space and time. God as presented by the theologian has in reality not a supernatural quality, but *more* natural ones. (p. 58)

In so far as Feuerbach is objecting to any attempt to arrive at the notion of divine predicates by arguing that they are an extension of human predicates, he is quite correct. On the other hand these difficulties only arise when one assumes that the task facing one is that of establishing talk about the divine by some kind of inferential or analogical link with talk about the human and the natural. This assumption is central in Feuerbach, as central as it is in the reflections of the other writers we have considered. Yet, it is precisely this assumption which needs to be examined. What does it amount to when someone says that religious belief *must* be the product of projection?

If we think of the phenomenon of projection as something an individual does, Feuerbach's claim runs into the kind of difficulty we have already encountered in discussing Freud. If I say that a person's view of his father is the product of projection, I may mean that the way he sees his father is the result of how he would like his father to be or how he would like to be himself, rather than the result of observing his father. Here, my claim about this person's view of his father can be confirmed or refuted. If it is confirmed, there will be a contrast between how the son sees his father and how his father really is. In such contexts, however, it would be odd to claim that the son's view of his father must be a product of projection. One would refute such a claim by an appeal to the facts. But Feuerbach does want to say that all religious beliefs must be a product of projection. He does not allow any distinction between religious beliefs which can be so characterized and those which cannot be described in this way. Ultimately, as we shall see, this is due to the kind of factuality he wants to attribute to religious claims. The particular account he offers about beliefs being the product of unfulfilled wishes soon runs into difficulties. We have already seen how it is possible for a ritual to be the expression of a wish without involving any confused view that a purpose, thwarted in nature, has somehow been achieved by other means. To insist that this cannot be the case would be like arguing that when a lover smashes a photograph of his beloved, this can only be the expression of a wish if the lover believes that since his beloved is too far away to be harmed by physical means, he can produce this harm by smashing her photograph. Apart from difficulties such as these, Feuerbach would also be forced to recognize that, on many occasions, the expression of desires in religion have nothing to do with attempts to fulfil them. The confession of desires is an obvious example. Here, the desires are expressed, not because it is felt that in this way they will be fulfilled, but on the contrary, as an expression of shame and remorse for having desired their fulfilment. Again, desires may be expressed in prayer and ritual in order to come to terms with them, it being recognized that in this world there is no guarantee that such desires will be fulfilled. The point of the prayer or ritual need not be to fulfil these desires in some other realm, but a working out of a relationship with the divine through these desires.[3] This could be true, for example, in prayers and rituals concerning the dead. When Feuerbach says that 'The grave of man is the birthplace of the gods' he thinks that belief in the reality of the dead, as Kamenka puts it, 'expresses the wish that the dead were still alive' (p. 41). We have seen that rituals concerning the dead may express no such wish. On the contrary, the love and respect shown to the dead, and the reality ascribed to them, would make no sense if it were thought that the dead were still alive. It is precisely because they are dead that the attitudes towards them expressed in prayer and ritual make sense.

If one attacks Feuerbach in this way, one is exposing his essentialism, an essentialism comparable to that we found in Freud. Freud wanted to discover the essence of dreaming. Feuerbach wants to discover the essence of religion. Their all-embracing explanations are refuted by the facts. Yet, Kamenka argues, this is not fatal to the general approach to religion advocated by Feuerbach. Kamenka argues that despite the fact that Feuerbach added to man's possession of knowledge, will and love, his consciousness of being a member of a species, he nevertheless pays insufficient attention to the social character of human existence. Yet, even when these social characteristics are stressed, one must beware of essentialism. Relationships within the institution of the family cannot, as we have seen, bear the burden of explanation that Freud wanted to place on them.[4] Neither will it do to make everything depend on the Marxist claim that social dependence is a product of class oppression and the impersonal laws by which all classes in society are bound. In fact, Kamenka believes that this has played a comparatively small part in the development of religious beliefs. Yet, he argues, it deserves serious attention. No particular account of religion as the product of projection will account for all cases. What Kamenka doesn't question, however, is that religious belief is always the product of *some* kind of projection: 'Religion not only *is* anthropology, in order to perform its social function it *needs* to be' (p. 47). Religious belief can be explained in terms of the purposes it serves. These purposes cannot be explained in purely individualistic terms. The social context of religious belief must be taken into account. In many ways, this is illustrated most strikingly in the work of Durkheim. In considering the claim that religion is a social product, light is thrown on the notion of projection and on the claim that religious belief *must* be the product of projection.

Durkheim is opposed to accounts of religious belief that seek to explain it in terms of the psychological abberations of the individual:

> For this school does not seek to locate religions in the social
> environments of which they are a part, and to differentiate them
> according to the different environments to which they are thus
> connected. But rather, . . . its purpose is to go beyond the national
> and historical differences to the universal and really human bases
> of the religious life. It is supposed that man has a religious nature
> of himself, in virtue of his own constitution, and independently of
> all social conditions, and they propose to study this.[5]

This programme can never be a plausible one, since religion is not the product of an individual. A religion existed before the birth of the individual and will continue to exist after his death. He acquires his religion in the way he acquires his language, namely, by being born into a particular society. The institutions and traditions connected with religion cannot be explained solely, if at all, as the creation of the individual. Social practices are not to be explained in terms of basic psychological facts about the individual. On the contrary, the activities which an individual engages in, his hopes and fears, thoughts and plans, are only intelligible in the context of the society in which he lives. Among these social practices are those of religion. Furthermore, as Durkheim points out,

> 'There was no given moment when religion began to exist, and there is consequently no need of finding a means of transporting ourselves thither in thought. Like every human institution, religion did not commence anywhere' (p. 8). He concludes that 'It is inadmissible that systems of ideas like religions, which have held so considerable a place in history, and to which, in all times, men have come to receive the energy which they must have to live, should be made up of a tissue of illusions.' (p. 69)

This led Durkheim to say that the psychological explanation of a social phenomenon is invariably the wrong one.

Yet, it would be quite wrong to conclude from these remarks that Durkheim thought that religious beliefs could be accepted at face value. There is an important passage in the Introduction to his work which shows that this is far from Durkheim's intention:

> When only the letter of the formulae is considered, these religious beliefs and practices undoubtedly seem disconcerting at times, and one is tempted to attribute them to some sort of a deep-rooted error. But one must know how to go underneath the symbol to the reality which it represents and which gives it its meaning. The most barbarous and the most fantastic rites and the strangest myths translate some human need, some aspect of life, either individual or social. The reasons with which the faithful justify them may be, and generally are, erroneous; but the true reasons do not cease to exist, and it is the duty of science to discover them. (pp. 2–3)

Here we find the same distinction between the manifest content of religious belief and its latent content which, in this case, will be uncovered by sociology. When one does go below the religious symbol to the reality it represents, one finds it is society itself. Religion is in fact the worship of society. This is an extremely odd claim and it is not at all easy to understand why anyone should want to make it.

Part of the answer to the above question can be found in Durkheim's essentialism. He, too, wants to discover the essence of religion. He does not want to waste time considering the actual ideas which constitute various religious beliefs. When he asks how we are to discover the meaning of religious beliefs he replies,

> Surely it is not by observing the complex religions which appear in the course of history. Every one of these is made up of such a variety of elements that it is very difficult to distinguish what is secondary from what is principal, the essential from the accessory. Suppose that the religion considered is like that of Egypt, India or the classical antiquity. It is a confused mass of many cults, varying according to the locality, the temples, the generations, the dynasties, the invasions, etc. Popular superstitions are there confused with the purest dogmas. Neither the thought nor the activity of the religion is evenly distributed among the believers; according to the men, the environment and the circumstances, the beliefs as well as the rites are thought of in different ways. Here they are priests, there they are monks, elsewhere they are laymen; there are mystics and rationalists, theologians and prophets, etc. In these conditions it is difficult to see what is common to all. In one or another of these systems it is quite possible to find the means of making a profitable study of some particular fact which is specially developed there, such as sacrifice or prophecy, monasticism or the mysteries; but how is it possible to find the common foundation of the religious life underneath the luxuriant vegetation which covers it? How is it possible to find, underneath the disputes of theology, the variations of ritual, the multiplicity of groups and the diversity of individuals, the fundamental states characteristic of religious mentality in general. (p. 3)

Durkheim never asked himself whether it made sense, or whether it was profitable, to look for the essence of religious belief. This was something he took for granted. And the essence of religion which he offers us is the worship of society. Durkheim wants to move from the premiss that religion is a social phenomenon, to the conclusion that religious belief has society as its object. On the face of it, this is an extremely odd argument, since it reverses the proper relation between various social movements and the notion of society. We can only explain what we mean by a human society by reference to the various ways in which different movements develop and influence each other. Durkheim, where religion is concerned, seems to want to explain a social movement by reference to the notion of society. Speaking of the notion of allegiance to the totem and social organization in totemic terms, Durkheim says of the relation between the totem and the social group governed by it,

> It is its flag; it is the sign by which each clan distinguishes itself from the others, the visible mark of its personality, a mark borne by everything which is a part of the clan under any title whatsoever, men, beasts, or things. So if it is at once the symbol of the god and of the society, is that not because the god and the society are only one? How could the emblem of the group have been able to become the figure of this quasi-divinity, if the group and the divinity were two distinct realities? The god of the clan, the totemic principle, can therefore be nothing else than the clan itself, personified and represented to the imagination under the visible form of the animal or vegetable which serves as totem. (p. 206)

Putting aside the empirical inaccuracies of Durkheim's theory, this again is an extraordinary argument in which what needs the closest questioning is presented as self-evident. In answer to the question how the emblem of a group can be thought of as divine, the reply could be, Because it was thought worthy of worship. Further, if a group is governed by its relation to certain religious symbols, then it is a religious group. Wherein lies the mystery? If a society is dominated by certain religious, moral, or political beliefs, it certainly does not follow that the content of such beliefs will refer to something called 'society' which has a reality independent of them. But this is how Durkheim wants to argue. The content of the beliefs which predominate in a society is of secondary importance to him. Such beliefs, however diverse, all serve a common function, namely, to underline and perpetuate social solidarity. Durkheim agrees with the other writers we have considered in thinking that believers are in the grip of delusions if they think that their rites and rituals are causally efficacious. These observances are efficacious, but their efficiency consists in strengthening social bonds: 'The moral efficacy of the rite, which is real, leads to the belief in its physical efficacy, which is imaginary' (p. 359). Again, Durkheim reverses the logical priority in the relations he is considering. He wants to argue that the ideas people share in a society, the beliefs they hold, can be explained in terms of the common social bonds they create. What he fails to recognize is that the common social bonds are only intelligible in terms of the common ideas, beliefs and activities people share. It will not do to argue, as Durkheim does, that the feeling of social solidarity engendered depends 'upon the fact that the group is assembled, and not upon the special reasons for which it is assembled' (p. 386).

If one tries to think of situations which would correspond to the above description, what comes most readily to mind is the hysteria of mass meetings. There are times when Durkheim's arguments seem dangerously close to this. Speaking of the social pressure an individual may feel operating on him, Durkheim says that its intensity is its moral ascendency. In other words, Durkheim does not analyse the influence of, say, moral norms in terms of their moral content, but, rather, he analyses the moral authority of the norms in terms of the intensity of their social influence and pressure. In this way, Durkheim's analysis impoverishes the whole idea of moral traditions which make an independent contribution to the life of a society. Durkheim's analysis would fit the case of an individual who conformed to certain norms of behaviour because of social pressure. Yet, he intends it to be an analysis of situations in which a person adheres to and shares these norms of behaviour. Such a person too, according to Durkheim, is simply expressing social solidarity. His analysis can take no account of the fact that people are related differently to the same norms of behaviour. Furthermore, solidarity is achieved, not by people sticking together for the sake of solidarity, but by their common regard for certain values, beliefs, standards, etc., etc. It is precisely when questions of solidarity become ends in themselves that the solidarity of the group or institution in question is beginning to weaken. We say that it is important that we stick together only when there is a danger that we are falling apart. The life of a family, a literary tradition, religious orthodoxy, etc., etc. are not maintained by those who participate in them making social solidarity or the maintenance of common bonds their aim. On the contrary, they remain united, or they have things in common, precisely in so far as they have a regard for other things for their own sakes. Durkheim says that

> When men of an inferior culture are associated in a common life,
> they are frequently led, by an instinctive tendency, as it were, to
> paint or cut upon the body, images that bear witness to their
> common existence . . . the early Christians painted on their skin
> the name of Christ or the sign of the cross; for a long time, the
> groups of pilgrims going to Palestine were also tattooed on the
> arm or wrist with designs representing the cross or the monogram
> of Christ . . . twenty young men in an Italian college, when on the
> point of separating decorated themselves with tattoos recording,
> in various ways, the years they had spent together. The same fact
> has frequently been observed among the soldiers in the same
> barracks, the sailors in the same boat, or the prisoners in the same
> jail . . . Its object is not to represent or bring to mind a determined
> object, but to bear witness to the fact that a certain number of
> individuals participate in the same moral life. (p. 236)

Remember, however, that the unity of this moral life is analysed by Durkheim in terms of feelings of solidarity and confidence. In the examples he offers above, Durkheim does present instances of common testimony, but it is a testimony to values of comradeship, the meaning of which varies with the context in question. They are not all examples of some one thing, namely, expressions of social solidarity, since, until some specific context is mentioned, that notion is quite empty. It only has a meaning for us when mentioned in abstraction because we are already acquainted with the kind of examples which would give it content. Durkheim, however, tries to argue that the specific allegiances can be understood only in so far as they are seen to serve the common function of expressing and experiencing social solidarity. Thus, he is able to ask,

> What essential difference is there between an assembly of
> Christians celebrating the principal dates of the life of Christ, or of
> Jews remembering the exodus from Egypt or the promulgation of
> the decalogue, and a reunion of citizens commemorating the
> promulgation of a new moral or legal system or some great event
> in the national life? (p. 427)

In this question resides the impoverishment of social movements which results from accepting Durkheim's arguments and a puzzle concerning the specific treatment of religious belief in this context.

As a result of his enquiries, Durkheim wanted to conclude that, from 'the fact that a "religious experience", if we choose to call it this, does exist and that it has a certain foundation ... it does not follow that the reality which is its foundation conforms objectively to the idea which believers have of it' (p. 417). The reason for this conclusion is that since all mythologies are expressions of one reality, society, 'Religious forces are therefore human forces, moral forces' (p. 419). These conclusions are Feuerbachian in spirit, but they pose a puzzle with regard to the treatment of religion found in both Feuerbach and Durkheim. The conclusions Durkheim draws are reductionist in character: religious beliefs cannot say what they want to say; their real function is to express something else. Yet, the puzzle is this: why should this argument have particular application to religion? As we have seen, as far as Durkheim was concerned, the same analysis applies to moral and political ideas. So if religious beliefs cannot say what they want to say, neither can moral or political beliefs. The function of all these beliefs is to express and make possible an experience of social solidarity. Yet, we have seen that what Durkheim has to say about the relations between particular social movements and traditions and the notion of society is radically confused. His analysis of these relations reverses the logical priority which they exemplify. But if we agree that his analysis is confused, it is only as confused in relation to religious movements and traditions as it is in relation to movements and traditions of any other kind. Therefore, if someone still wants to present a reductionist account of religious belief, despite admitting the confusions involved in Durkheim's discussion of social movements, some additional arguments have to be found for treating religion in this way. It is clear, then, that the answer to the question why people have thought that *religion* must be the product of projection need not lie in the kind of analysis offered by Durkheim. The answer must lie elsewhere.

The same puzzle confronts us when we look back to Feuerbach. Feuerbach wants to argue that all we talk about intelligibly is to be found within human experience. But why should this in itself have any adverse consequences for the claims of religious belief? The fact that language is spoken by men does not entail the conclusion that when men speak they always speak about man. This no more follows than the conclusion of the argument that because human traditions and movements are social in character, they must have 'society' as their object. We have already concerned ourselves with the confusions in the latter argument, but they are not dissimilar from the confusions involved in the former argument. The language in which men talk about trees, birds, beauty, ugliness, is, of course, the language of men, but it does not follow because of this that when men talk of such things they are really talking about human nature, or that such things are the creations or projections of men. Yet, Feuerbach does want to say that man created God in his own image; that religious belief is the product of projection. But if he wants to say this, it cannot be simply because God is spoken of in human language, since this is true of many things other than God which Feuerbach would not want to call the products of projection. Again, if we want to find the reason why Feuerbach and Durkheim thought that religious belief must be the product of projection, we must look further.

In order to find the answer to our question we need to return to the beginning of this chapter and to Kamenka's remarks about the relationship between Feuerbach's enquiries and the eighteenth-century Enlightenment. Kamenka tells us that Feuerbach thought that the task of showing that there is no God had already been accomplished. His work was to bring out the nature of the confusion involved in the error of belief. In a revealing footnote, Kamenka makes the following remark:

> Only when such analysis becomes a *substitute* for considering the truth or falsity of a belief does it become vicious. The two questions—'why does a man have a certain belief?' and 'is that belief true?' are separate issues and must be kept distinct. If the distinction is maintained, however, the first question is as legitimate as the second. In particular contexts (especially where the belief is patently false), this first question may be much more interesting and we may come to understand the nature of an error much more precisely by understanding how men are led into it. (p. 160)

The interesting question, here, is what *would* have to be the case for Feuerbach, or for Kamenka for that matter, for a religious belief to be true? Or what would Kamenka mean if, as I suspect, he described religious belief as patently false? I think that both Feuerbach and Kamenka would mean that an entity, called God, does not exist. In other words, they both accept the terms of reference set by Hume for a discussion of whether God exists. Similarly, I suspect that when Durkheim denies that 'religious experience' conforms objectively to reality in the way believers would have us believe, he has in mind the denial that this experience refers to any existent entity called God.

Kamenka keeps insisting that theology finds itself in a contradictory state of affairs. If it presents God as supernatural, it presents a being who is indescribable and of no interest to human beings. If, on the other hand, God is presented as a natural God, the belief can be analysed in purely human terms without any supernatural residue. Kamenka argues in this way because he says, in the spirit of Feuerbach, that 'Man gets the ideas contained, rearranged and elaborated in religion precisely where he gets all other ideas—from human experience' (p. 59). In a footnote to this remark, Kamenka shows how Feuerbach was influenced by the implications of Hume's philosophical legacy:

> Here again Feuerbach is unconsciously echoing one of the basic positions put in Hume, which Feuerbach came close to probably indirectly, through the influence of French materialism: 'Nothing is more free than the imagination of man, and though it cannot exceed that original stock of ideas, furnished by the internal and the external senses, it has unlimited power of mixing, compounding, separating and dividing these ideas, in all the varieties of fiction and vision. It can feign a train of events with all the appearance of reality, ascribe to them a particular time and place, conceive them as existent, and point them out to itself with every circumstance, that belongs to any historical fact, which it believes with the greatest certainty'—Hume, *Enquiry Concerning Human Understanding*, Section V, ii. (p. 166)

Yet, all the assumptions which Kamenka advances uncritically can, in fact, be questioned.

First, we have already seen in numerous examples that the relation of a believer to various rituals and rites need not be explicable in terms of his unfulfilled wishes. Thus, Kamenka's conclusion that Feuerbach's general position is confirmed by the fact that religion loses its hold on an area as soon as a man ceases to feel helpless in it, is a falsification of the facts. It distorts other possible relations that a man may have to natural objects that he worships, and the reasons why religion may lose its hold when man's causal control of these objects increases. We saw, in Chapter Three, that religious beliefs need not be regarded as supplementary methods for attaining causal efficacy and that neither need the erosion of such beliefs be accounted for in terms of their comparative inefficiency as means of bringing about such ends. Thus, even when the natural is made the object of worship, such worship need not admit the kind of analysis offered by Feuerbach and endorsed by Kamenka.

Second, what if Hume's assumptions about the reality of God are mistaken? What if talk about a supernatural being does not entail the problematic inference from the world to God which, as we have seen, gives rise to insurmountable logical difficulties? What if talk about the supernatural does not entail the postulation of two worlds, one of which is beyond the one we know in the sense Hume found so objectionable? What if talk of being in the world and yet not of it does not entail the kind of dualism that Feuerbach found so objectionable?

But how are these questions to be answered? Surely, by looking at the role which such ideas have in the context of religious belief. If Feuerbach wishes to stress that all language is human language, all well and good. Within that language men talk of God. Let us therefore look at such talk, but without assuming, as Feuerbach did, that Hume's terms of reference for such an investigation must be accepted *ab initio*. If Durkheim wishes to stress that religion is a social movement, all well and good. Let us therefore look at the ideas which characterize that movement and not assume that they are of secondary importance, an assumption based on the further assumption that such ideas must be treated in a Humean fashion. Let us rather consider, open-mindedly, Simone Weil's remark that

> The French school of sociology is very nearly right in its social explanation of religion. It only fails to explain one infinitely small thing; but this infinitely small thing is the grain of mustard seed, the buried pearl, the leaven, the salt. This infinitely small thing is God; it is infinitely more than everything.[6]

If Kamenka wants to suggest that Feuerbach's observations indicate the type of approach to religion which is desirable, then he cannot say, as he does, that the word 'model' does not stand in need of further analysis for his purposes. On the contrary, his assumption that one needs a model of a reductionist character in order to explain the errors involved in religious belief is one that can be subjected to criticism, even if it is admitted that the variety of religious pheno-mena demands a wide range of such models. To begin with, the whole question of the relation between a model and social phenomena is a problematic one. Peter Winch has shown important differences between such attempts and the use of models in explaining natural phenomena.[7] If the fall of an apple is explained in terms of gravity, it is important to notice that the notion of gravity plays no role in the existence of the apple. The notion of gravity belongs to the physicist's method of representation. But when we come to an explanation of social phenomena, the situation is very different. Here we are considering the behaviour of people which is already rule-governed. If an account of this behaviour is to be acceptable, it must take account of the concepts at work in people's lives. The question which needs to be considered is whether religious concepts too have this internal relation to people's conduct in certain contexts. Kamenka, I believe, would deny that this is so, believing that religious beliefs are ideologies needing models to explain them. Yet, Kamenka takes this to be the case because he accepts Hume's terms of reference for the locating of religious concepts. Yet, Hume's terms of reference need to be questioned. Hitherto, we have been examining inheritors of Hume's legacy who, agreeing that there are logically insuperable barriers to talking of a God beyond the world we know, have offered explanations of religion as a human product. In these explanations, religious belief, it was argued, was shown to be a mistake. Marett and Freud argued that the mistakes themselves were products of deeper emotional stress. We have found difficulties in all these views, but it would be premature to conclude that it makes no sense to speak of religious beliefs as confused. This is because all confused beliefs are not the products of mistakes. Metaphysical beliefs, while not mis-taken, are the product of confusion. It has been argued recently that to understand religious beliefs an analogy should be sought between them and metaphysical beliefs. We turn to an examination of this analogy in the next chapter.

NOTES

1. Eugene Kamenka, *The Philosophy of Ludwig Feuerbach*, p. 37.
2. Ludwig Feuerbach, *The Essence of Christianity*, p. 23.
3. For an extended treatment of this question see my *The Concept of Prayer*, Ch. 6.
4. Ultimately, as we saw in the last chapter, Freud cannot be credited with an insight into the primacy of the social in understanding human behaviour. His final appeal is to an individualistic psychology of a static kind.
5. Emile Durkheim, *Elementary Forms of The Religious Life*, Bk. 1, Ch. 4 pp. 94–5.
6. Simone Weil, 'A War of Religions', in *Selected Essays*, p. 215.
7. See Peter Winch, *The Idea of a Social Science*.

H

Seven
Religion, Magic and Metaphysics

One of our main concerns since Chapter Two has been to question whether philosophical discussions of religion are predestined to fall prey to the objections raised by Hume in his *Dialogues Concerning Natural Religion*. This concern, however, can be easily misunderstood. It is not a concern to defend religion against objections which would entail atheism. Rather, the point of the enquiry is to become clear about the kind of language involved in religious beliefs. It is often said that religious beliefs are metaphysical beliefs. Various metaphysical beliefs claim to give an account of religious beliefs, but the latter existed without any knowledge of the former. Nevertheless, it may be said that metaphysical beliefs are latent in religious beliefs. When these metaphysical beliefs fall in face of philosophical criticism, then, many would argue, religious beliefs fall with them.

Metaphysics goes too far; it is an attempt to say what cannot be said. For example, the metaphysician wants to move from asking for the cause of some particular thing or event to asking for the cause of everything. But the notion of the cause of everything is a confused one. When one looks at religious beliefs one finds a belief in God as the creator of everything. Philosophers have assumed that belief in such a creator has, as one of its preconditions, the intelligibility of the notion of a cause of everything. But that notion is unintelligible. Thus, the fall of a metaphysical notion heralds the fall of a religious belief. But the confusion resides in equating metaphysical and religious beliefs. In this chapter I shall argue that despite prima-facie resemblances between metaphysical and religious beliefs, the differences between metaphysical and religious beliefs are far more important than these similarities.

As we have seen, confronted by religious and magical beliefs, anthropologists and philosophers alike have asked, 'What are these?' and have thought that an answer has been found in explanations of them as attempts to control natural processes by supernatural means.

We have seen that this answer has been influential, not only in anthropology, but also in philosophy where its influence is still strong. The spirit of the answer is well expressed in the following remarks by Frazer:

> But reflection and enquiry should satisfy us that to our predecessors we are indebted for much of what we thought most our own, and that their errors were not wilful extravagances or the ravings of insanity, but simply hypotheses, justifiable as such at the time they were propounded, but which a fuller experience has proved to be inadequate. It is only by the successive testing of hypotheses and rejection of the false that truth is at last elicited. After all, what we call truth is only the hypothesis which is found to work best. Therefore in reviewing the opinions and practices of ruder ages and races we shall do well to look with leniency upon their errors as inevitable slips made in the search for truth, and to give them the benefit of that indulgence which we ourselves may one day stand in need of: cum excusatione itaque veteres audiendi sunt.[1]

In striking opposition to this way of thinking, Wittgenstein in his 'Remarks on Frazer's *The Golden Bough*', shows how religious and magical beliefs can be misunderstood if they are thought of as mistaken factual hypotheses or as elementary conceptions of causal connections. In his Introductory Note to the 'Remarks' Rush Rhees tells us that Wittgenstein wrote them 'partly from an interest in "the mythology in our language"', and that 'He wanted to show that certain familiar expressions belong to mythology, just as certain transitions or moves we make in speaking do. He does this by showing their kinship with moves and expressions in magical practices or ritual—if we recognise this kinship, the ritual observances become intelligible—we do not need to ask why they happen.'[2] In our discussions throughout this book we have argued for a similar conclusion. Given this conclusion, one cannot draw a close analogy between religious beliefs and metaphysics, since in the case of metaphysical beliefs we do want to ask why they happen. Wittgenstein seems to have thought, however, that the intelligibility of ritual observances could be brought out by emphasizing an analogy between magic and metaphysics. Rhees tells us that he began an earlier version of the first set of remarks with the words:

I think now that the right thing would be to start my book with remarks on metaphysics as a kind of magic.

In which I must neither speak in favour of magic nor make fun of it.

The deep character of magic would have to be preserved. (p. 19)

Rhees points out that in the published 'Remarks' Wittgenstein does not treat metaphysics as a kind of magic, but he is suggesting that magic and metaphysics can be compared. My difficulty is that I do not see how such a comparison could bring out the intelligibility of religious or magical beliefs or bring out the depth in them.[3]

By comparing religion and magic with metaphysics one can show that religious and magical beliefs are misunderstood if they are thought of in general as mistakes or errors. We have seen in Chapters Four and Five, however, that it does not follow from this conclusion alone that magic and religion cannot be thought of as confusion of another kind. On the contrary, as I hope to show, the comparison with metaphysics encourages one to move in the direction of thinking otherwise. The comparison may show that magic and religion cannot be thought of as confusion of a certain kind, but it does not show that they cannot be thought of as confusion of any kind.

These conclusions will be argued for in this chapter. In the first part of the chapter, I mention four prima-facie similarities which encourage us to compare religion and magic with metaphysics. In the second part of the chapter I show how, trading on these resemblances, an argument can emerge which concludes that all distinctively magical and religious beliefs are the products of confusion. In the final part of the chapter I argue that this argument is based on a misunderstanding, a misunderstanding which can be emphasized by showing that there are radical differences between religion and magic on the one hand, and metaphysics on the other, and that on the whole the analogy between them is best avoided.

Why should anyone want to compare religion and magic with metaphysics? There are at least four prima-facie resemblances which might lead one to do so.

The first prima-facie resemblance can be brought out by emphasizing a common assumption often made about metaphysical, religious and magical beliefs which is mistaken. It is thought that these beliefs are factual hypotheses. When someone says that I can only be certain of my own sensations, when a believer says that God cares for us all the time, or when we hear of a ritual which is meant to protect the living from the ghosts of slain warriors, we may react to all of them as if they were factual mistakes. On the other hand, we run into trouble once we try to treat them in the ways we would treat such mistakes.

We may wonder how a person got himself into a state where he thought that he could only be certain of his own sensations. Is it not a simple matter to point out to him that he is in fact certain of many things: his name, where he lives, that there are trees, flowers and birds in his garden, and so on for a thousand instances? If he is sane enough he has to admit that he is as sure of these things as the next man. Yet, as we saw in the opening chapter, the matter is not so simple as that. If we are saying that the metaphysician is a person who is uncertain when he ought to be certain, how do we account for the fact that his conduct betrays no signs of uncertainty? On a walk through the town with him, twists and turns, nods and responses, perceptions and actions, show no uncertainty on his part. Neither, clearly, is the metaphysician like the poor madman who has lost all sense of certainty. On the contrary, any normal person accompanying him on a walk will testify that he is as sane as the next man. Furthermore, if we say that the metaphysician is uncertain when he should be certain, how is his uncertainty to be remedied? Since the kinds of uncertainty we understand are readily connected with, and make a difference to, our attitudes and behaviour in a variety of situations, we can indicate, at least in principle, what would have to be done to settle the uncertainty. If I am uncertain about whether I have enough money to pay for a meal, I can check how much money I have before entering the restaurant. But if, having been wined, dined, and had the meal paid for, by our metaphysician, he tells us that he cannot be certain that he has done any of these things, there is nothing in the series of events that I can point to in order to show him that he was certain of these things after all. Since his so-called uncertainty is asserted in the absence of those features of a situation which give talk of uncertainty its sense, I cannot resort to such features of the situation in an attempt to settle his uncertainty. The metaphysical doubt lacks the kind of surroundings which give ordinary doubt its sense. It is held in face of any possible state of affairs other than my own sensations, and is not revisable by the discovery of new facts as ordinary doubts would be. The metaphysician is not making a remark which is subject to familiar forms of verification and falsification which enter into what we mean by making sure. He seems to be saying that given all these factors one still should not say that one is certain of anything except one's own sensations. His thesis is essentially one about what it makes sense to say about certainty; it is not a thesis about what is the case.

Appreciating the above characteristic of metaphysics, some people have talked of the metaphysician's conclusions as stipulations. The metaphysician, without realizing it, is making a stipulation or recommendation that the word 'certainty' shall only be used with reference to one's own sensations. The trouble with this reaction is that it seems to rob metaphysics of its depth. Metaphysics seems to be an arbitrary affair. One feels like saying that the metaphysician does not choose to make a recommendation, but is driven to his conclusion. If one asks what it is that drives him to these conclusions, one is concerned with the relation of the metaphysical conclusion to the reflections which surround it. But the description of the metaphysical conclusion as a recommendation does not bring out the source of the temptation towards that conclusion.

The sources of temptation in this context are many. In the case we are considering, someone may feel that only his sensations are certain because he feels that there is something about them which marks them off from everything else. He may have been impressed by the fact that we can be mistaken about other people's sensations. I may say to someone who is holding the side of his face. 'I see your toothache has returned', to which he may reply, 'No, I'm afraid it's become a mannerism.' Here there is a use for such expressions as, 'I thought he was in pain, but I was wrong.' On the other hand, there is no use for such expressions as 'I thought I was in pain, but I was wrong'. Of course, it does not follow from these distinctions that one can never be certain that another person is in pain, but the metaphysician does not realize this. Indeed, he may not be aware that such distinctions constitute one of the reasons why he has come to his conclusions about certainty. When such distinctions are made explicit to him in argument, he may come to see that all that follows from them is that if I say that I know that another person is in pain it always makes sense to ask me how I know, whereas it makes no sense to ask that question if I say that I am in pain.

The point of these observations is simply to give one brief example of what is meant by saying that the resolution of a metaphysical claim does not depend on the discovery of new facts, but rather on assembling reminders from what we already know. If I am uncertain about how many horses are running in the next race, what I need is more information, more facts. If I say that I can only be certain of my own sensations, the 'can' refers to what I think it makes sense to say about certainty. The resolution of this question is not determined by more facts, but by reflecting on the ways we speak about certainty in a variety of contexts. Similarly, when we consider the notion of a cause of everything, what we need is not a more thorough empirical investigation, but an investigation into what it is that makes us want to speak in this way. To treat a metaphysical claim as though it were an hypothesis about the facts is to misconstrue its character.

Those who want to draw an analogy between metaphysics, religion and magic will point out that one also misconstrues the character of religious and magical beliefs if one thinks of them as mistaken hypotheses about the facts. On such a view, the mistake involved in the belief that a certain event is a curse by the ghosts of the slain would be pointed out by showing that the ghosts were not responsible for the event. The mistake involved in saying that God cares for us all would be brought out by showing that the facts, particularly the evil in the world, do not justify this conclusion.

Yet, as in the case of the metaphysical utterances, the relation of the magical and religious beliefs to the facts is not as straightforward as one might think. One soon finds that given that the ritual concerning the dead warriors has not been observed, any ensuing misfortune will be attributed to the ghosts of the slain. As far as the facts are concerned, the warrior may see no more than we see. If a rock falls on him, we may feel quite satisfied with the explanation of how the rock came to be dislodged and of how the warrior happened to be passing by at that moment. Yet, he wants to add, whereas we might not, that all this is due to his being in disfavour with the ghosts of slain warriors. This further belief, however, cannot be falsified. One cannot conduct a test whereby one observes whether everyone who does not perform the required ritual satisfactorily is dogged by misfortune. It may be said that the misfortune is to come later, or, if it never comes, that his ghost in turn will know no rest, and so on. Clearly, then, if two people disagree over whether misfortune is due to the ghosts of slain warriors, they are very unlike two people who disagree over whether a nephew's misfortunes are due to a scheming uncle. But, similarly, if two people disagree over whether good fortune is due to God's care, they are very unlike two people who disagree over whether a nephew's good fortune is due to a benevolent uncle. One cannot establish any statistical correlation between the fortunes of those who do and those who do not believe in God. Furthermore, believers often speak of God's care when others would regard such talk as madness. Job went as far as to say that even if God slew him, yet would he trust in Him. Some philosophers have found such remarks so hard to take that they have concluded that this must have been a piece of ironic blasphemy on Job's part, a blasphemy so well disguised that it has fooled the faithful down the ages.[4] Since the faithful speak of God's care even in adversity, there seems to be no possibility of securing evidence of God not caring. Thus, the religious belief, like the magical belief, seems unfalsifiable. The belief that one's life can be affected by the ghosts of the slain or the belief that God's care is over all, seems to have a kind of necessity such that the apparent contradictory of the belief is not even to be entertained. The beliefs seem to be ways of looking at fortune and misfortune rather than one way among many of explaining particular fortunes and misfortunes.

As in the metaphysical examples, the magical and religious beliefs are misconstrued if they are thought to be capable of falsification by appeal to factual evidence. What we need to do in order to bring out their force is simply to bring to bear on them other features of the lives of the people who hold these magical and religious beliefs. As in the case of the metaphysical beliefs, what we need is not more factual information, but a certain assembling of the material that lies before us. I shall say more about this later. At the moment I simply want to re-emphasize that the first reason why someone might want to stress an analogy between metaphysical, magical and religious beliefs is that none of these beliefs can be established or refuted by appeal to factual evidence.

The second prima-facie resemblance between metaphysics, magic and religion is that all three make a deep impression on us. We may not be able to formulate exactly why they should make such an impression on us, but we feel convinced that whatever is going on here it cannot be something trivial or insignificant. Furthermore, when a straightforward explanation, confirmation or refutation of the beliefs is offered, we feel that the depth associated with them has somehow slipped through our fingers. For example, if, in face of the metaphysical claim that we can only be certain of our own sensations, a person points out that it is refuted by the fact that he is certain about a thousand things, our response is 'Yes, but . . .' We feel that there is more to it than that, and, indeed, there is. Similarly, if someone wanting to refute the claim that misfortunes are due to the ghosts of the slain pointed out that there are perfectly good natural explanations of these misfortunes, or if someone wanting to deny that God cares for us all the time points to disasters and evils, and if it is said that in any case there is insufficient evidence to speak of there being any ghosts or gods in the first place, again our response might be, 'Yes, but . . .' The element of depth, what drew our attention to the magical and religious beliefs in the first place, seems to be missing from such explanations.

The third prima-facie resemblance between metaphysics, magic and religion follows from these reactions. As a result of such reactions it may be felt that whatever account one gives of metaphysics, magic and religion, it must preserve what is deep in them.

The fourth prima-facie resemblance which may make people endorse the analogy between metaphysics, magic and religion is that in all three one is concerned with limiting conceptions which determine what can and cannot be said in a given context. Normally, if we say that we are uncertain about something, it makes sense for someone to ask us to make certain about it. But in the case of the metaphysician who says that he can only be certain about his own sensations, we are asked how we can be certain after we have fulfilled what would normally be called making certain. The metaphysician attempts to go beyond the limits of what can be asked. He wants to ask what cannot be asked.

The belief that misfortune can be attributed to the ghosts of the slain, and that God cares for us all the time, are also limiting conceptions. They set limits on what it makes sense to say about one's misfortunes in certain contexts. The denial of such conceptions would be the denial of a whole way of looking at things, rather than a denial that so-and-so was responsible for one's fortunes or misfortunes; a denial which would have its place within customs of praising, blaming, ascribing responsibility, and so on.

Why, then, given these four prima-facie resemblances should one express caution about the analogy between metaphysics, magic and religion? The answer is that the main import of these resemblances is negative; we see how metaphysics, magic and religion are *not* to be understood. If one thinks of the analogy as a positive one, one may be led to conclude that magic and religion are forms of confusion. Let us now examine the route by which this conclusion is reached.

Undeniably, it is extremely important to show that magic and religion in general cannot be construed as a mistake or blunder. To think otherwise is to misunderstand the kind of activity one is concerned with here and the kind of language which characterizes it. So much can be appreciated by exploring prima-facie analogies between metaphysical, magical and religious beliefs. But what kind of language is involved in magic or religion? To show that magical and religious beliefs are not mistakes is not to show that they are free from confusion. On the contrary, it might be argued, it is necessary to see that magical and religious beliefs cannot be so construed in order to appreciate the kind of confusion involved in them. The analogy with metaphysics shows us why this is so. Metaphysical utterances cannot be regarded as empirical hypotheses, but that does not mean that they are free from confusion. As we have seen, this must be grasped in order to appreciate the character of the confusion involved. Might not the same be true of magic and religion? If there is something in our language which tempts us towards metaphysical conclusions, might there not be something in ourselves which tempts us towards magical and religious beliefs? When the prima-facie resemblances between metaphysics, magic and religion are emphasized to the extent of becoming a positive analogy, it is not hard to see how such an argument can emerge.[5]

When a man tells us that the misfortune which has befallen him is due to the ghosts of slain warriors, or that God cares for him all the time, it is difficult, as we have seen, to disprove this in the way one could disprove a similar allegation against a human being. The issue is complicated in that it is clear both that the person believes in some queer kind of causal connection between the slain warriors and his present misfortune, or between God and events in his life, and that the conditions needed to establish such a causal connection are manifestly absent. It is not surprising that any attempt to give a coherent account of his beliefs ends in confusion. He seems to be believing in the causal efficacy of some kind of agency although no sense can be made of his belief. Can a man believe what does not make sense? It is important here to resist the temptation to answer in the negative, just as it is important not to deny that the metaphysician means what he says. It is not that these people do not mean what they say. They do. The point to emphasize is that what they want to say cannot be said. Further, the reason why they want to say these things cannot be explained by revealing an error. One does the metaphysician an injustice if one thinks he is blind to facts that other people see. He is driven to his metaphysical conclusions because he half-perceives and misconstrues features of the language we share with him. Similarly, we may well do the believer in magic or religion an injustice if we think, as some of the early anthropologists tended to do, that he is blind to, or has an elementary understanding of, the causal connections the rest of us appreciate. The source of the trouble lies deeper in his hopes and fears. His beliefs about magic and religion are the product of his emotions.

But what is the connection between belief in God and human wishes; how is the heart linked with religion? Latent in this question may be the assumption that once the connection between religion and human desires is understood, religion would be seen to be an illusion. We discussed this assumption in Chapters Four and Five. Freud, in his analysis of illusions, saw that it was insufficient to think of them as mistakes or errors. He saw that it was essential to take account of the element of wishing in illusions; the wish that things might be so.[6] From such strong desires emanates the confused belief that things are so. The child, for various reasons, wishes so much for a land beyond the rainbow, that it comes to believe that there is a land beyond the rainbow.

Might not the same be true of magic and religion? A person may feel so guilty about the people he has slain and wish so much for a chance to right himself with them, that he comes to believe that though dead, they still exist. People moved by the imperfections of this world wish that things were different. Their desires are so strong that they come to believe that things will be different—that all will be rectified one day by a God who cares. Notice that there is a genuine depth in these beliefs. People who thought nothing of those they had killed, or of the evils of the world, would not be driven to them. Yet, because of the intensity of their emotions, the believers are driven too far. They are driven to thinking that God or the dead can actually affect the affairs of men. We are reminded of the metaphysician's urge to go too far, to ask whether we can be certain even after everything had been done which we would normally call making certain. We are also brought to see why it is that just because metaphysical, magical or religious utterances cannot in general be construed as factual mistakes, it does not follow that they are not products of confusion. In the case of the metaphysician the sources of the confusion can be found in the language he uses and which we share with him, whereas in the case of the believers the sources of confusion are in their hopes and fears, hopes and fears that we share with them.

It is no part of my intention to deny that the argument that I have outlined in this part of the chapter has any application. No doubt there are instances of beliefs which are called magical or religious to which it would apply. We can mark the distinction either as one between magic, religion and superstition, or say that not all beliefs which are called magical or religious are of the same kind. The important point is simply that we do draw a distinction. Wittgenstein draws it as follows:

> We should distinguish between magical operations and those operations which rest on a false, over-simplified notion of things and processes. For instance, if someone says that the illness is moving from one part of the body into another, or if he takes measures to draw off the illness as though it were a liquid or a temperature. He is then using a false picture, a picture that doesn't fit.[7]

It seems to me that the most one can achieve by a comparison between metaphysics, magic and religion is to throw light on the logic of superstition. Superstitions are not adequately accounted for as errors or mistakes. The connection between superstitions and our hopes and fears cannot be ignored. The lover wishes to see his lover to such an extent that he becomes convinced that he will see her again, though she is dead. Examination of the particular case may show it to be a superstition. Nothing I go on to say in this chapter is meant to deny that possibility. All I am saying is that when light is thrown on such possibilities as these, light is not necessarily thrown on magic and religion at the same time.

We have seen that by emphasizing an analogy between metaphysics, magic and religion, light can be thrown on the logic of superstition.

Yet, not all magic or religion is superstition. Why, it might be asked, should a philosopher want to point this out? Were it not for the current misleading talk about 'Wittgensteinian Fideism' it ought to be clear that marking such differences has nothing to do with a desire to justify magic or religion (whatever that might mean). The reason lies rather in a desire to bring out the character of the language involved in certain areas of human discourse. If this is misconstrued we also misconstrue what it is to say something in these contexts and the kind of limit one finds in the language concerning what it does and does not make sense to say. All this is quite neutral with respect to whether one finds religion or magic attractive or repugnant, or whether one should like to see, or try to do something about, such beliefs increasing or diminishing.

In this final section of the chapter I want to show how severely limited are the prima-facie resemblances between metaphysics, magic and religion if what we want to achieve is an understanding of magical and religious beliefs. One can see this by noting six important differences between metaphysics on the one hand and magical and religious beliefs on the other.

The first difference is related to the first prima-facie similarity we have noted. We saw that metaphysics, magic and religion are misunderstood if they are treated as mistakes or blunders concerning the facts. We saw that all we need do in order to bring out the force of these beliefs was to arrange what already lies before us in a certain way. Yet, the prima-facie similarity can take us no further without misleading us. This is because the relation of a metaphysical con-clusion to the language that surrounds it is radically different from the relation of a magical or religious utterance to the language that surrounds it. When these relations are made explicit we see that the metaphysical conclusion is a product of confusion about the grammar of our language. The argument we considered in the second part of the chapter and which was discussed at greater length earlier in the book, seeks to draw the same conclusion about magic and religion in general. This cannot be done. Where the magical or religious utter-ance or practice is not superstitious, the relation of the utterance or practice to the language surrounding it is simply an expression of its force. Thus, the practices of a warrior tribe, the values associated with battle, the status of the slayer and the slain, all give point to the practice of appeasing the souls of slain warriors and to the belief that failure to honour them leads to misfortune. What believing that God cares for us all the time amounts to varies with different circumstances. The circumstances bring out the force of the belief. This can be illustrated by an example I have used previously.[8] Suppose one witnesses a child falling overboard. One is unsure of one's chances of saving him or of surviving the effort to do so. Suddenly, one may say to oneself, 'Jump! Trust in God!' This expression need not be connected with a belief that some supernatural agency is going to guarantee the safe return of either the child or oneself. No, it is a matter of not putting oneself first, weighing up the pros and cons. One gives oneself to what has to be done. It is this giving of oneself without reserve—trusting it—which gives force to the expression 'Trust in God' in this context. In the case of metaphysical beliefs, the language surrounding them helps one to understand why one is tempted to a confused conclusion. In the case of magic and religion, the surrounding context is not the source of their confusion, but the source of their life and force.

The second radical difference between metaphysics and magical and religious beliefs is simply a consequence of the first. Once the relation between a metaphysical conclusion and its surroundings is recognized, one can no longer hold on to the metaphysical conclusion. According to the argument outlined in the second part of the chapter the same consequence should follow in the case of magic and religion. Once one could bring someone to see that his fear of the dead is a product of his exaggerated fear about his past misdeeds, he could then retain a responsible sense of guilt and at the same time be rid of his fear of the dead. Once one could get someone to see that his belief that God watches over us is a product of his desire that things should be other than they are in this life, he would be able to take the rough with the smooth realistically. But given our non-superstitious sense of magic and religion, making the relation between them and their surroundings explicit can hardly lead to abandoning them since one would be simply bringing out their force.

In the differences between metaphysics and magical and religious beliefs that we have noted so far, we have concluded by referring to bringing out the force of magical and religious beliefs. But what does this 'bringing out' consist in? According to one of the prima-facie resemblances we noted, any account of magic, religion and metaphysics must preserve the depth involved in them. Once again, however, this prima-facie resemblance may mislead us. Rush Rhees says that

We cannot answer metaphysical questions by any theory, scientific or historical... If we think we can, we have not understood the kind of questions they are, the kind of difficulty expressed by them. When Wittgenstein says that any attempt to find a *theory* of the magic and ritual practices is futile 'since we have only to bring together and arrange in the right way what we *know*' (i.e. what is not hypothesis or conjecture) 'without adding anything, and the satisfaction... comes of itself'—he would say that this is also the method we have to follow in philosophy, in discussing the problems of metaphysics. (p. 20)

But we have seen that this prima-facie resemblance is strictly limited. The consequences of bringing together what we already know are radically different when we compare metaphysics with magic and religion. Differences seem far more important than similarities in this context.

In the case of metaphysics we saw that as a result of bringing together what already lies before us, the metaphysical conclusion is shown to be confused. How, then, can metaphysics also be deep? One answer is that the depth is in the problem to which the metaphysician is offering an answer. As Rhees puts it, '...it is the *problems* that are deep in the way that magic is, and they make us uneasy in much the same way. The problems, not the solutions offered. We cannot ignore the solutions—the metaphysical statements and systems—because it is these that show us what the difficulties (or problems) are' (p. 24). If we have never felt the temptation towards these metaphysical conclusions ourselves, never felt the force of the attraction, it is unlikely that we shall appreciate the depth of the problems they are meant to answer. Still, when one does see the depth and character of the problem, one will not hang on to the metaphysical conclusion. Yet, despite the fact that one might have to conclude that the metaphysical conclusion is confused, one could also say that what the metaphysician is concerned with is deep.

Things are rather different in the case of the argument we considered in the second part of the chapter. Here, too, there is a bringing together of what we already know in order to explain why, for example, a person fears the dead or thinks that God watches over him. In this context also we can recognize that something deep is involved without denying that it issues in confusion. One could say that the very depth of a man's guilt or of a man's desires drove him to excess in what he says about God and about the dead. A psycho-analyst, for example, might say that deep problems led to a distorted belief. If the man is to carry on normally, without the loss of what is important in his life, the depth of his problems must be retained, but his distorted beliefs dispensed with.

When we turn to magical and religious beliefs which are not superstitious, the question of the relation of the belief to that which surrounds it is importantly different. In the case of metaphysics and certain superstitions one is able to draw a distinction between the depth of the problems which led people to metaphysical or super-stitious conclusions on the one hand, and the confusion in those conclusions on the other. No such distinction is possible with the kind of magic and religion we now have in mind. The magical and religious practices are related to what surrounds them, but not in such a way as makes us conclude that they are confused in any way. Wittgenstein refers to these surroundings as follows:

> That a man's shadow, which looks like a man, or that his mirror image, or that rain, thunderstorms, the phases of the moon, the change of seasons, the likelinesses and differences of animals to one another and to human beings, the phenomenon of death, of birth and of sexual life, in short everything a man perceives year in, year out around him, play a part in his thinking (his philosophy) and his practices, is obvious, or in other words it is what we really know and find interesting.
>
> How could fire or fire's resemblance to the sun have failed to make an impression on the awakening mind of man? But not 'because he can't explain it' (the stupid superstition of our time)— for does an 'explanation make it less impressive?' (pp. 32–3)

We may not find these features of human life impressive any more, but, the people who did were not confused in any way. The magical and religious beliefs or practices are not the confused outcome of deep problems and emotions, but are themselves expressions of what went deep in people's lives. That a man's misfortunes are said by him to be due to his dishonouring the ghosts of slain warriors is itself the form that depth takes here; it is an expression of what the dead mean to him and to the people amongst whom he lives. That a man says that God cares for him in all things is the expression of the terms in which he meets and makes sense of the contingencies of life.

Of course, there is nothing inherently deep in the form of words in which a magical or religious utterance is expressed. The depth comes from the lives of the people in which such utterances play a part. The same words in the mouth of another person or in a different context might simply be trivial. Yet, given that the magical or religious utterance does have a depth in the lives of people, it may still be true that what the utterance says cannot be said in any other way. Rush Rhees asks:

> But when you say that these people fear the ghost of the slain, what *are* you saying? Can you explain except in mythology? If Frazer had said that in some tribe when a warrior kills an enemy he fears the *corpse* of the slain, there would not be this question. But that is not what he wants to say here. (p. 21)

In the case of metaphysics and superstition or neurosis the recognition of what is deep involves no longer being in the grip of the metaphysical or superstitious statements, although they may be mentioned. In the case of magical or religious beliefs and practices the recognition of what is deep *is* the recognition of the role which these beliefs and practices have in people's lives.

The fourth difference between metaphysics and magic and religion is closely connected with the conclusions we have just reached. While the metaphysician clings to his system and conclusions we cannot say that he has attained the understanding of his problem open to him. While the neurotic or superstitious person clings to his beliefs he cannot be said to possess the understanding of his situation open to him. To possess this understanding they must give up that which grips them. On the other hand, one cannot say anything like this about magical or religious beliefs. To suggest that understanding can only be achieved if the magical or religious beliefs and practices are given up is itself a form of confusion.

The fifth difference between metaphysics and magical and religious beliefs concerns the sense in which the notion of a conceptual limit is connected with them. In the case of metaphysics we saw that we are tempted to go beyond the limit of what can be said. Similarly, it may be said that the superstitious or neurotic person is driven to go beyond what it makes sense to say or to do. Magic and religion, on the other hand, are themselves, in certain forms, expressions of the limits of sense. In the examples we have chosen, the magical rituals

I

concerning dead warriors set the limits concerning what can be thought of life and death in battle; belief in God's care likewise sets limits on what can be said about fortune and misfortune. The values expressed in such magical rituals have just as real a connection with the lives of the people concerned as the techniques of warfare. If these people have a deep concern about the way in which dead warriors are thought of, this cannot be separated from what the dead are to them. If the dead were dishonoured in any way this would not simply be a matter of regret, but of terror. Any misfortune which befalls them is understood in the light of this relationship with the dead. It is in this sense that magical rites set limits to people's thinking, to what people think it appropriate, proper or reasonable to think. There need be no implications in these beliefs which involve any kind of theory concerning causal relations between the dead and events in people's lives. All one can say is that fortunes and misfortunes are given a sense in that way, that is all.

A belief in God's care in all circumstances in no way conflicts with practical measures to change circumstances for the better, and is just as real as such measures to the believer. After showing how God could be said to speak to an individual even through madness, Drury raises the question of whether it is right to apply electric convulsive therapy to such patients: 'Are they not sometimes at least a gross interference with what should be left to the wisdom of God? Are we always right to use them?'[9] Drury's reply is an example of what belief in a God who watches over all things can mean to one who is nevertheless engaged in changing the mental and physical circumstances of people's lives:

> Of course we are. A doctor who tries to prolong life and ease the pains of the dying in no way detracts from the majesty and significance of death. A doctor who attempts to shorten and relieve the suffering of the mentally ill in no way diminishes the lesson of madness. If we are to take the doctrine of the creed seriously, 'by whom all things were made', then we must accept that madness in all its horror is as much part of God's creation as the tubercle *bacillus* and the cancer cell. We do not know why these things should be, and if we did they would not be what they are. We are right to fight against them with all the energy and all the weapons that we have. For this energy and these weapons

are also part of His creation. But this we must never forget, good physical health, good mental health are not the absolute good for man. These can be lost and yet nothing be lost. The absolute good, the goal and final end of our being is in heaven and not here; and all earthly things as though they get us but thither.

And so to all of us, in sickness or in health, in sanity or in madness, in the vigour of youth or in the decrepitude of senility, God speaks these words which He spoke once to St Augustine:

Currite, ego feram, et ego perducam, et ibi ego feram.

Run on, I will carry you, I will bring you to the end of your journey and there also will I carry you. (p. 137)

The difference I am stressing can be emphasized by pointing out that in the case of superstition or neurosis, if one wants to do something about them, the task is one of bringing persons back from superstition or neurosis to normality. As we have seen in Chapter Five, Freud, who thought of religious belief as a neurosis, expressed the matter exactly in these terms. He spoke of reversing the animistic process and of putting back into the human mind the structural conditions which primitive man had transposed into the external world.

Although there are extremely important differences between the import of Freud's remarks and the following comment by Wittgenstein on the treatment of metaphysical questions, nevertheless, they have in common the assumption that certain forms of confusion can be cleared up by contrasting the confusion with normality and showing the routes by which the confusion gets a grip on us. 'Our task', Wittgenstein tells us, 'is to bring words back from their metaphysical to their everyday use.'[10] One of the essential differences between metaphysics, superstition and neurosis on the one hand,[11] and magic and religion on the other, is that one cannot say that our task is to bring words back from their magical and religious to their everyday use. My aim has been to show that in certain contexts the magical and the religious *is* the everyday use.

This brings us to the sixth and final difference I want to mention in contrasting metaphysics with magical and religious beliefs. It concerns the different ways in which the questions, 'Why is he speaking like that?' or 'What is it to say that?' enter into accounts of these beliefs. This has close connections with the question of the limits of what can and cannot be said, together with the question of what treatment of these limits one can expect to find in philosophy.

We saw in the treatment of our metaphysical example that one can be led to ask how we can be certain of something beyond the stage where it makes sense to do so. Part of the trouble with the person who says that he can only be certain of his own sensations is precisely this. He has to deny, for example, that we can be certain whether the room next door is occupied even after we have found out, by means which we would normally describe as making certain, that it is. When he realizes where the source of his reluctance lies, he comes to see that we can retain important differences between statements about my own sensations and statements about other people's sensations while still asserting that we can be certain about the latter. He can be brought to see that it only makes sense to say that we are uncertain about something if we know what it means to call something certain. If he wants to ask why we call *that* making certain, the answer is that we do, that is all. Here, further questioning would be pointless. My purpose here is not to rehearse the arguments in detail, but simply to note the point at which the question, 'What is the point of saying that?' or 'Why do you speak like that?' stops. The initial metaphysical statement that I can only be certain of my own sensations is questioned. One can ask, 'Why do you speak like that?' My point is that in the resolution of the metaphysical puzzle one will come to ways of speaking, for example, ways of making certain, where it makes no sense to ask, 'Why do you speak like that?'

Similar conclusions can be drawn from the treatment of neuroses or extreme superstitions. Initially, such behaviour certainly poses the question, 'Why is he saying this?' or 'Why is he doing this?' The aim of anyone who wants to rid a person of neurosis or superstition is to get him back to normality. This notion of normality contains difficulties which I cannot discuss here. Again, I simply want to note the fact that on many occasions when cure or release has been attained, it will make no sense to ask, 'And why do you call that normality?'

When we turn to the magical or religious beliefs and practices, I suggest that the matter is different. If my previous arguments are sound we should see that the magical and religious beliefs, unlike the metaphysical statement, the neurosis or the superstition, are not forms of language of which it makes sense to ask, 'Why are you speaking like that?' but are themselves forms of language about which it makes no sense to ask such questions. When one comes to the point in one's account where one says that the dead are thought of in a certain way, or that fortune and misfortune are met in a certain way, it would be confused to continue by asking why people think in this way. Of course, one might be able to give an historical account of the development of these beliefs, but that would not be an account of the impressiveness of the thoughts. We might also bring out the force of the thought by putting something alongside it which may be effective. But the 'something' one puts alongside it is not an explanation: it has no parallel with putting things alongside metaphysical or superstitious statements in order to bring out the confusion in them. Wittgenstein shows us the sense in which the force of a ritual can be brought out without offering an explanation of it. He refers to Frazer's telling of the story of the King of the Wood at Nemi:

> Put that account of the King of the Wood at Nemi together with the phrase 'the majesty of death', and you see that they are one.
>   The life of the priest-king shows what is meant by that phrase.
>   If someone is gripped by the majesty of death, then through such a life he can give expression to it.—Of course this is not an explanation: it puts one symbol in place of another. Or one ceremony in place of another.[12]

Rhees says that in the early remarks on Frazer, 'once one has given such an exposition and arrangement, once he has "shown what there is", then, Wittgenstein thought, the philosopher must "retire" and say nothing. Either the other man will begin to see how it is, or, if he does not . . . there is nothing we can do about it' (p. 25). Rhees goes on to say that there are difficulties about this, difficulties concerning what 'arranging the material' in this context amounts to, or what is to count as 'the right way'. This is especially true when the magical belief or religious practice one is trying to elucidate or understand belongs to a culture other than one's own. He expresses the difficulty by asking, 'Granting that ritual is a language, how should I understand the ritual-language of peoples of such widely different cultures, in different parts of the world, just from what I find in my *own* language?' (p. 25). In the later remarks on Frazer we do not get this emphasis on one's own language, but rather on what

is deep in the life of a people. There are problems about what understanding involves in this context, but I cannot pursue them now.[13]

In any case, these difficulties do not affect my main point which is
that many magical and religious beliefs are limiting conceptions,
forms of language which do not invite the question, Why do you say
that? or Why are you speaking like that? Unlike the statements
of metaphysics and superstition, many magical and religious beliefs
and practices do not await a further analysis which is supposed to
bring a greater clarity, in the light of which one can no longer hold
on to the beliefs and practices in their original form. On the contrary,
as I have tried to argue, magical and religious beliefs are themselves
expressions of limits concerning what it does and what it does not
make sense to say. But if one asks what these beliefs say, the only
answer is that they say themselves. What they say may be elucidated
in the ways I have noted, but it cannot be explained. Faced with
such uses of language 'We can only *describe* and say, human life is
like that' (p. 30).

The conclusions of this chapter illustrate the philosophical programme facing anyone who wishes to deny that Hume's terms of
reference are essential for an understanding of religious belief. Before
considering specifically religious beliefs this programme can be
advanced by an examination of beliefs which, perhaps more than
most, seem predestined to fall foul of Hume's criticisms, namely,
beliefs concerning the reality of the dead.

NOTES

1. James Frazer, *The Golden Bough* (abridged ed.), p. 264.
2. Rush Rhees, Introductory Note to Wittgenstein's 'Remarks on Frazer's
   The Golden Bough', p. 18.
3. Nevertheless, for the extent to which Wittgenstein may have wanted to
   press an analogy between magic and metaphysics see my paper, 'Wittgenstein's Full Stop', forthcoming in the Proceedings of the University
   of Western Ontario Wittgenstein Colloquium, 1976.
4. Hermann Tennessen, 'A Masterpiece of Existential Blasphemy', in *The
   Human World*, No. 13, 1973.
5. An argument of this form appears in a paper by my colleague H. O.
   Mounce, called, 'Understanding a Primitive Society', *Philosophy*, October
   1973.
6. Freud, *The Future of an Illusion*.
7. 'Remarks on Frazer's *The Golden Bough*', p. 31.
8. D. Z. Phillips, *The Concept of Prayer*, p. 124.
9. M. O'C. Drury, 'Madness and Religion', in *The Danger of Words*, p. 137.
10. Ludwig Wittgenstein, *Philosophical Investigations*, I, 116.

11. This is not meant to deny important differences between metaphysics and neurosis. If one calls metaphysics confused, the source of the trouble is in the language; it is not personal, whereas the trouble in a neurosis is.
12. Ludwig Wittgenstein, 'Remarks on Frazer's *The Golden Bough*', p. 30.
13. Much of the recent discussion concerning such problems has surrounded Peter Winch's paper, 'Understanding a Primitive Society'. In the last part of the paper Winch discusses how one's understanding is extended in understanding practices in cultures other than one's own.

Eight
Perspectives on the Dead

Hume's view of the way in which human knowledge depends on our original stock of ideas rules out any postulation of a world other than or beyond the familiar surroundings in which we live our lives. If one had to think of an example which would call forth the full severity of Hume's criticisms, one would be hard pressed to think of a better example than various beliefs about the reality of the dead. Yet, it is such beliefs that I want to discuss in this chapter.

To many contemporary philosophers, to discuss the reality of the dead is an unpromising enterprise. In their opinion, to speak thus is at best a piece of obscurantism and mystification, and at worst self-contradictory. Behind these philosophical claims, it is said, lies an unavoidable truth which inspires them with unshakeable confidence: the dead are dead. What, then, are we to make of beliefs which talk of the reality of the dead? The answer to this question is one with which we have become familiar during the course of this book: people's desires have got the better of them. Although the dead are dead, people, for a variety of reasons, wish that things were otherwise. Worse, an alarmingly large number of people have convinced themselves, in one way or another, that things are otherwise. They talk of eternal life, life beyond the grave, of the dead being with us, of communion with the dead, messages from the dead, the ghosts of the dead, or the dead meeting each other, and so on. Philosophers are not immune to these tendencies in human nature, and so it should not surprise us to see them trying to find room in their speculations for such flights of the imagination. Yet, it is argued, in face of all such attempts to ascribe reality to the dead, common sense demands the reiteration of the simple, but far from homely, truth: the dead are dead, and that is all there is to say about it.

But is that all there is to say about it? Those influenced by Hume would have us believe that the statement, 'The dead are dead' has the role of rejecting various beliefs about the dead. In this chapter I shall argue that, in certain circumstances, that statement, while it may disagree with other beliefs about the dead, is itself one such belief. Such a conclusion, were it established, would constitute an attack on Hume's assumption that those who talk about the reality of the dead postulate a world beyond human experience, whereas those who say that the dead are dead are free from such a dubious dualism. It would show that those who speak of the reality of the dead and those who insist that the dead are dead share the same language, but take up different perspectives within it.

These conclusions will not be acceptable to the inheritors of Hume's philosophical legacy. They will appear to them as extraordinary claims. They will want to insist that 'The dead are dead' is not a belief about, or a perspective on, the dead at all, but simply the re-emphasis of a familiar fact, a fact which, for various reasons, people do not want to face up to. The statement of this fact can be distinguished from all beliefs about the reality of the dead. These beliefs are the products of illusion. Further, the statement seeks to rid our lives of fantasy by calling attention to the obvious.

How does fantasy get a grip on us where beliefs about the dead are concerned? One might cite as an instance the example Wisdom discusses at the beginning of his paper, 'Gods':

A child may wish to sit a while with his father and he may, when he has done what his father dislikes, fear punishment and feel distress at causing vexation, and while his father is alive he may feel sure of help when danger threatens and feel that there is sympathy for him when disaster has come. When his father is dead he will no longer expect punishment or help. Maybe for a moment an old fear will come or a cry for help escape him, but he will at once remember that this is no good now. He may feel that his father is no more until perhaps someone says to him that his father is still alive though he lives now in another world and one so far away that there is no hope of seeing him or hearing his voice again. The child may be told that nevertheless his father can see him and hear all that he says. When he has been told this the child will still fear no punishment nor expect any sign of his father, but now, even more than he did when his father was alive, he will feel that his father sees him all the time and will dread distressing him and when he has done something wrong he will feel separated from his father until he has felt sorry for what he has done. Maybe when he himself comes to die he will be like a man who expects to find a friend in the strange country where he is going. . .[1]

Wisdom's example contains all the assumptions which are dear to the writers we have discussed and to the inheritors of Hume's philosophical legacy. The child holds a belief which is patently false: he believes his dead father is still alive. Next, we are shown the nature of his error by seeing the way fantasy brings it about. The movement of thought seems to be as follows: The child's life is full of the father. The father's pleasure and displeasure are everything to him. Then the father dies. Thus, to use Simone Weil's language, a void is created. But the child is told that his father is still alive, although he cannot be seen or heard because he now lives in a far-off world. Imagination fills the void and, as a result, the father's will governs the child of faith once again.

On the basis of this account of the genesis of beliefs concerning dead fathers, certain general conclusions, as we have seen, can be drawn. First, it has been assumed that beliefs concerning the reality of the dead must be a means of filling a void; in this case a void created by bereavement. Second, it has also been assumed that beliefs concerning the reality of the dead can only fill the void created successfully if they convince the believer that the person thought to be dead is in fact still alive. In this way one can establish the conclusion that beliefs in the reality of the dead are patently false, and that the genesis of such beliefs reveals the fantasies by which they were created. In this chapter, however, I shall argue that the two assumptions on which this conclusion is based are, in fact, false. I shall begin by considering the second assumption, namely, that beliefs in the reality of the dead can only fill a void created by bereavement if they convince the believer that the person thought to be dead is, in fact, alive.

In Wisdom's example the void is filled by the imagination. By this I mean first and foremost that the void is filled by the consolation of an imaginary state of affairs, namely, the continued existence of the father. There is something that the child cannot accept and the imagination is all too ready to compensate his loss. Philosophers, who, at this point, emphasize that the dead are dead, want to remind us that because of the void that loss of contact creates, there is a danger that desire may determine reality. The child wants the loved one to exist so much that when told of the far-off world he eagerly accepts the good news. He believes the loved one exists because he wants the loved one to exist. In this way, there is a loss of contact with reality. Beliefs may be based on such a loss of contact and when this is so philosophers are right in pointing this out. But need a belief in the reality of the dead which is a response to a void created by bereavement involve the conviction that the one thought to be dead is still alive? Simone Weil shows us that this need not follow. She is aware that a loss of contact with reality may occur in such situations, but she is also aware of other possibilities:

> ... To lose somebody: we suffer at the thought that the dead one, the absent one should have become something imaginary, something false. But the longing we have for him is not imaginary. We must go down into ourselves, where the desire which is not imaginary resides. Hunger; we imagine different foods; but the hunger itself is real; we must seize hold of the hunger.
>
> The loss of contact with reality—there lies evil, there lies sorrow. There are certain situations which bring about such a loss: deprivation, suffering. The remedy is to use the loss itself as an intermediary for attaining reality. The presence of the dead one is imaginary, but his absence is very real; it is henceforth his manner of appearing.[2]

Peter Winch comments on these remarks as follows:

> Suppose that the dead person is a woman whom I deeply loved; that while she lived, this woman was the centre round which the world revolved as far as I was concerned: anything that I thought worth doing, anything in which I took an interest, was connected in my thoughts in some way with her. I may say, 'The world without her is impossible for me to live in. The only thing from which I could draw any support is lacking'. Simone Weil says that 'The remedy is to use the loss itself as an intermediary for attaining reality'. That is to say, I must look for what *is* real in my situation—for the centre from which I am now forced to view the world. And this, she suggests, is to be found in my very loss, my longing, in the void created by the beloved's absence.
>
> It is important to what Simone Weil is saying that longing is intentional. I long *for* something or someone. In other words my

longing itself, which is undoubtedly something real, cannot be grasped except as a longing for that person. So mention of her is essential to describing the reality of the world as it is for me; she has *not* become something unreal, imaginary, because mention of her is indispensible to describing the world as it is. Her absence is, henceforth, 'her way of appearing'; she makes a difference to the world by virtue of her absence.[3]

There is clearly a marked difference between Simone Weil's remarks and Winch's comments on them on the one hand, and Wisdom's example of the child's belief on the other hand. In both cases a void is present, a void created by death. In Wisdom's example, the void has to be filled, while in Winch's example, the void is not filled, but faced. For Wisdom's child the recognition of the void is equivalent to recognizing that the father is no more. Once the father had filled the child's world. After the father's death, despite occasional impulses of thought in which the child believes the father to be still at hand, the child realizes that to think that the father can still be part of his world is no good now. How can the father be part of his world when the father is no more? There is no suggestion in Wisdom's example of the dead making a difference to one's world by virtue of their absence. The only way in which the child's father comes to play a part in his world again is by the arrival of unexpected news: things are not what they seem, the father still lives in another world. One can see without too much difficulty why many would want to mark the difference between the two examples by noting the presence of fantasy in the one and its absence in the other. In Wisdom's example there is a loss of contact with reality, whereas in Winch's example it is precisely reality that is embraced, despite the fact that the reality to be embraced is the longing for a dead one and the realization that the dead can only be present, in this context, in the form of absence. Now it may be thought that the fact that the father is necessarily absent from this life in Wisdom's example makes the difference between it and the case Winch discusses minimal. This would be to ignore a radical discontinuity present in the one case and absent in the other. In Wisdom's example, the death of the father clearly has consequences for the child's life: he no longer expects punishment or help. When he is told, however, that his father is still alive in another world, Wisdom tells us that now, 'even more than he did when his father was alive, he will feel that his father sees him all the time and will dread distressing him and when he has done something wrong he will feel separated from his father until he has felt sorry for what he has done'. He is related *even more* to his father now in certain respects than he was before. The difference is simply a difference of degree. True, there are no actual helps or punishments, but this is simply because death has placed such a distance between himself and his father so as to make this impracticable. The point could be expressed in this way: the child has not come to have a relation with a dead father, he simply intensifies a prior relationship with a father who still lives, although afar off. Apart from the unavoidable absence, the relationship has the same character as it had previously. Absence has made the heart grow fonder. If, on the other hand, one tries to apply this analysis to Winch's example, one blurs the distinction between fantasy and reality. Winch emphasizes that the longing caused by bereavement is a longing for a particular person, 'so that mention of her is essential to describing the reality of the world as it is for me'. That is to say, part of how the world is for me is determined by the absence of a loved one in a way in which it obviously would not be if I had not given the dead one a second thought. If, however, I begin to think that the loved one is still alive, I lose contact with reality, that is, with the reality of her death, and I am led into different kinds of false expectations and consolations. Consider the difference between how, after the death of a loved one, a favourite café table at which one used to sit with her can acquire new significance,[4] and one's beginning to think that one will meet the loved one again at that table, that one can actually see her waiting for one at the table, or that at some distant place, unreachable except by death, she too sits waiting for her loved one to join her. In the first case what happens can be described as one way of coming to terms with the void created by the death of a loved one, whereas in the other reactions what happens can be described as a failure to come to terms with the death of a loved one, a failure which appears in fantasy.[5] Such fantasies may end in tragedy.

In her short story, 'The Lame Shall Enter First', Flannery O'Connor tells of the relationship between a widower, Sheppard, and his young son, Norton. Sheppard is the director of a recreation centre and a part-time social worker. His mother's death has created an enormous void in the life of the young boy, but the father thinks that the boy's grief is too extreme, even irrational. Instead of moping listlessly about the house he should be getting down to making

something of his life. In this respect he compares him unfavourably
with a lame delinquent called Johnson whom he befriends. When
Sheppard reflects on the boy's adverse background, he is convinced
that something can be made of him, something which his own son,
with all his advantages, could not attain. He gives Johnson more and
more attention, finally bringing him into his own home. He is ap-
palled to find that Johnson is in the grip of the irrationality of
religion, explaining his behaviour by saying that he is in Satan's
power. He promises Johnson to explain his devil to him. On one
occasion, when the boy is accused of arson and later cleared, the
social worker's remorse for having thought him guilty is intense.
After that, he steadfastly believes in his innocence despite other
charges made against him. When Johnson is alone with the young
son, however, he reveals his true attitude to Sheppard: '"God, kid,"
Johnson said in a cracked voice, "how do you stand it?" His face was
stiff with outrage. "He thinks he's Jesus Christ!"' He talks to the
son about his religious ideas, about the way in which good people
go to heaven and wicked people go to hell. He tells Norton that if his
mother was a good woman she now exists on high. Norton is anxious
to know where that is. '"It's in the sky somewhere," Johnson said,
"but you got to be dead to get there. You can't go in no space ship".'
The father tries in vain to destroy these ideas, but they are a source
of consolation to the young boy, his only contact with his mother.
Johnson, because of his interest in astronomy, has been given a
telescope which is lodged in the attic. It becomes linked in Norton's
mind with his mother who exists on high. At one stage, Sheppard
finds his son in the attic convinced that he has located his mother.
He tells his son that the telescope cannot show him anything but
star clusters. But the child is waving his arm: '"She's there!" he
cried, not turning around from the telescope. "She waved at me!"'
At the end of the story we find that Johnson has been fooling
Sheppard all along. He has been guilty of everything he has been
accused of and tries to implicate the social worker. He is taken away
by the police compounding lie on lie. The story draws to its close
with Sheppard reflecting on his actions:

'I have nothing to reproach myself with,' he began again. 'I did
more for him than I did for my own child.' He heard his voice as
if it were the voice of his accuser. He repeated the sentence silently.
Slowly his face drained of colour. It became almost grey beneath

the white halo of his hair. The sentence echoed in his mind, each syllable like a dull blow. . . He had stuffed his own emptiness with good works like a glutton. He had ignored his own son to feed his vision of himself. . .

He saw Norton at the telescope, all back and ears, saw his arm shoot up and wave frantically. A rush of agonizing love for the child rushed over him like a transfusion of life. The little boy's face appeared to him transformed; the image of his salvation; all light. He groaned with joy. He would make everything up to him. He would never let him suffer again. He would be mother and father. He jumped up and ran to his room, to kiss him, to tell him that he loved him, that he would never fail him again.

The light was on in Norton's room but the bed was empty. He turned and dashed up the attic stairs and at the top reeled back like a man on the edge of a pit. The tripod had fallen and the telescope lay on the floor. A few feet over it, the child hung in the jungle of shadows, just below the beam from which he had launched his flight into space.[6]

Here, the way in which imagination fills the void leads to tragedy. The child's love for his dead mother is real enough, but the meeting he seeks with her is all too like a meeting in this life. It can be sharply distinguished from Simone Weil's discussion of the sense in which the dead can be present in the form of absence. Yet, it is Flannery O'Connor's story and Wisdom's example which fulfil the conditions of those who argue that belief in the reality of the dead must entail belief in another world which is a product of our un-fulfilled wishes in this one. But from the comparison of the examples provided by Wisdom, Winch and Flannery O'Connor's short story, we can see that if someone were to suggest that to speak of the reality of the dead is necessarily to involve oneself in fantasy, his suggestion would be false. He would be blind to certain possibilities, possibilities which have been described as the dead being present in the form of absence. So far from being identifiable with fantasy, such examples have been distinguished from fantasy. Furthermore, these examples show that belief in the reality of the dead does not pre-suppose, as Wisdom's example would have us conclude, a belief that those we thought were dead are in fact still living.

Where fantasy fills the void philosophers may want to remind us that the dead are dead. But we have seen that, contrary to the assumptions often made by such philosophers, in face of the void created by the death of a loved one, belief in the reality of the dead need not entail an attempt to fill the void by convincing oneself that the one thought to be dead is still alive. Therefore beliefs in the reality of the dead need not entail beliefs which are patently false.

In the previous section we saw now it is possible to have beliefs about the reality of the dead without being committed to the belief that those who have died are still alive in another realm. Yet, despite these conclusions, the philosophers who wish to insist that the dead are dead need not be unduly perturbed. Of course, they would have to admit that coming to terms with a void created by death need not involve one in fantasy. There are more ways of facing the void than simply recognizing that the dead are dead. The dead one, as we have seen, may become present for someone in the form of absence. This is not an instance of filling a void but of facing it, and it is not the product of fantasy.

Yet, so far we are dealing with a human attitude to the dead. We are still far from beliefs which ascribe eternal life to the dead and speak of the dead meeting each other or watching over the living. Here we seem to be referring to a supernatural world beyond the familiar world we know. It is such beliefs, many philosophers would argue, that are the product of fantasy; a fantasy created in an attempt to fill a void. But need these beliefs be reactions to a void at all? It must be admitted that despite the differences between Wisdom's and Winch's examples, it remains true that a void created by bereavement remains central to an understanding of both of them. Even when a void is faced rather than filled, the way in which it is faced cannot be understood without reference to the void itself. Nevertheless, we cannot conclude from this that the beliefs we now want to consider must be reactions to a void. On the contrary, in discussing them we shall have reason to doubt the other assumption made concerning perspectives on the dead, namely, that they *must* be related to a void created by death to be intelligible.

Undoubtedly, for Wisdom's child of faith, the possibility to live under the eye of a father who has died, to dread distressing him and to feel separated from him until he feels sorry for a wrong he has done, all depends on his belief that his father is still alive in another world. The father's will that he strives to live by in his absence is of essentially the same character as the will of the father when they lived together. Death, in this instance, does not affect the character of the will. This is not true in other examples of the will of the dead. In these, the fact that the will one is talking about is the will of the dead affects what we mean by 'will'. In particular, it often seems that the reverence for the will of the dead is not a reaction to a void created by bereavement. Kierkegaard discusses some examples of this kind in *Purity of Heart*.

At this point in the book Kierkegaard is discussing the self-deception involved in willing the good out of fear of punishment. More particularly, he is discussing the form such self-deception takes when one wants to ingratiate oneself with someone one respects. Moral integrity can thus become subordinate to other considerations:

> The living person may perhaps favour you too much—perhaps too
> little. If you see him each day, your shame will perhaps lose
> something of its intensity or perhaps bring on itself an acute
> disease, so that you would wish to possess a magic means of
> receiving the revered one, so that you wished to be able to
> ingratiate yourself with him or by any means to raise yourself up in
> his good graces, because his judgement has become for you the
> most important thing of all. How much danger and temptation to
> double-mindedness![7]

Kierkegaard says that this danger is not entirely absent until, as far as moral considerations are concerned, one can bring oneself to view the living as if they were already dead. Why does Kierkegaard make such an extraordinary claim? He has in mind the fact that one cannot argue with the dead; one either comes to terms with them or one does not. Kierkegaard wants to bring out an analogy between the unconditional demands of morality and the unchangeableness which death brings about—the will of the dead is fixed, unchanging. When the dead person is connected in the mind of the living with certain moral ideals, contemplation of the dead may act as a paradigm of submission to unconditional moral demands. One can argue with a living person, hope to get him to change his mind, accuse him of being mistaken, and so on. But it is not so with the will of a dead person since it does not exist in an earthly sense. It is, to use Kierkegaard's phrase, a transfigured will:

> One who is living can indeed be mistaken, can be changed, can be

K

stampeded in a moment and by the moment... A man cannot get round a transfigured one. Favour and persuasion and overhastiness belong to the moments of earthly life. The departed one does not notice these appearances, the transfigured one cannot understand them. (pp. 80–1)

These remarks can be taken as grammatical remarks about the will of the dead. They set limits to what, in certain contexts, it makes sense to say about the dead. Once this is recognized, the difference between Kierkegaard's example and Wisdom's example becomes apparent. All we need imagine is a practice among a people where the dead are regarded in the way Kierkegaard depicts. Clearly, where the dead are worthy of such consideration there is no question of the attitude to the dead being the result of reaction to a void created by death. On the contrary, the attitude belongs to the status that the dead have among the living. The attributes of the living which are worthy of admiration or emulation become fixed in death, unchanging sources of contemplation for the living. The will of the living becomes transfigured in death.

At first it may seem that there are similarities between Kierkegaard's and Wisdom's treatment of perspectives on the dead. Kierkegaard tells us that 'the transfigured one exists only as transfigured, not visibly to the earthly eye, not audibly to the earthly ear' (p. 81). We may be reminded that Wisdom's child of faith is also told that although his father is still alive in another world, 'there is no hope of seeing him or hearing his voice again'. Do these remarks amount to the same thing? I think not. One must bear in mind the logical continuity involved in Wisdom's example. As far as one can tell, there is no suggestion that the father exists in another world in any sense other than he existed in this life. Although the child is described as living according to his father's will, there is nothing in Wisdom's example to suggest that the father, in the other world, could not be mistaken, stamped in a moment or by the moment. The reason why I say this is because, as we have seen, it is essential to Wisdom's child of faith to believe that his father is *still alive*. Death, in Wisdom's example, has brought about a separation, but no transfiguration. There is no suggestion in Kierkegaard's example that the father is still alive in another world, a suggestion to which continuity of the same mode of existence is essential. He says emphatically that 'the transfigured one exists only as transfigured'. It would make sense for Wisdom's child to argue with his far-off father, although no answer would be forthcoming. Things would have to be settled at a future meeting when he meets him in that far-off land. Such possibilities are ruled out in Kierkegaard's example. To argue with a transfigured one is to cease to regard him as a transfigured one:

> He cannot be changed, not in the least particular, without its being instantly noted, and without all being lost, and without his vanishing. The transfigured one exists only as transfigured. He cannot be changed into anything better. He is the transfigured one. He cannot be altered. He is indeed a departed one. He remains true to himself, one and the same—this glorified one! (p. 81)[8]

The contrast between the two examples could hardly be greater. For Wisdom, it is the possibility of regarding the dead as though they were still alive which makes a certain kind of faith possible. For Kierkegaard, on the other hand, in a sense already discussed, it is the possibility of regarding the living as if they were already dead which makes certain ethical relationships with other people possible. These relationships, however, depend on the dead having a certain status. The dead person in death, with respect to certain moral ideals, no doubt imperfectly followed in this life, is transfigured, glorified, or, one might say, raised up on high. That which is sown corruptible is raised incorruptible. Wisdom in his example endeavours to convey the fixed and unchanging character of the father's will, but fails to do so because of his insistence that the father is still alive. The fixity and unchangeableness he tries to capture elude him because he pays little attention to the evaluative notions of transfiguration, glorification, and raising on high, in connection with the dead. Kierkegaard, rightly, makes these central in his discussion of these questions.

A consideration of Kierkegaard's example shows us that belief in the reality of the dead need not be a response to a void created by death. The status of the dead in the eyes of the living can itself constitute what is involved in belief in the reality of the dead. Thus, Marett points out that within animism one has the following distinctions with respect to the reality of the dead:

> A yam lives without intelligence, and therefore has no *tarunga* or 'soul'. A pig has a *tarunga* and so likewise has a man, but with

this difference that when a pig dies he has no *tindalo* or 'ghost', but a man's *tarunga* at his death becomes a *tindalo*. Even so, however, only a great man's *tarunga* becomes a *tindalo* with *mana*, a 'ghost of worship'. (p. 117)

A plant is not thought to be a proper object of certain relationships and attitudes—it has no soul. Men and animals are proper objects of moral concern. They share a life which has many things in common. Yet, only a human life, it may be thought, when it is over, has a fixed eternal significance for the living, a life on which judgement can be passed. Further, the lives of holy people, when they pass into eternity, become objects of contemplation and worship. The lives of the ancestors are the fixed points which give meaning to the existence of the living.

Such beliefs cannot be explained in terms of emotional needs which, it is alleged, give rise to them. Instead of being understood as a projection made in time of stress or in the grip of the illusion that a situation uncontrollable by other means is now being brought under human control, these beliefs can be seen as the measure by which people think of and assess their relationships to other people and the states of their own souls. Later in his article Wisdom is tempted to see the genesis of the belief in the dead father in a certain light:

When a man's father fails him by death or weakness how much he needs another father, one in the heavens with whom is 'no variableness nor shadow of turning'. (p. 165)

For Wisdom's child of faith, belief in the second father is a product of the void created by the death of the first. The first father fails the child by dying. In his need, fantasy fills the void, and he believes that his father still lives in another world. In Kierkegaard's example, belief in the reality of the dead is not the product of anything. As we have said before, if there were no earthly fathers it is hard to see how one could have the notion of fathers in heaven. Nevertheless, it in no way follows from this that beliefs concerning the latter are products of tension concerning the former. Such beliefs will, of course, be related to people's lives in a variety of ways, but no explanation of the beliefs can be given which reduces them to fantasies born of prior conditions. If one asks why people should believe in the reality of the dead, why the dead should be held in awe, reverence or dread, one can only reply that people *do* react to the dead in this way, that is all. By assembling certain material which surrounds the beliefs, and by apt comparisons, one may be able to bring out the force of the beliefs. That would be an elucidation of the beliefs, not an explanation of them. The kind of belief Kierkegaard is talking about cannot be explained away. The belief cannot be reduced to something more fundamental than itself. It is the belief that is fundamental.

Someone might ask how, in a given instance, one is to determine whether a belief one is confronted by is a belief in the reality of the dead or the product of fantasy. There is no general answer to this question. One's answer will depend on an examination of the particular case, on the sentiments and expectations involved. The same form of words may hide very different cases. 'My father watches over me' may be an instance of the kind of example Kierkegaard is discussing; or it may be nearer to Wisdom's example. No doubt the character of many utterances will be mixed, making any clear answer impossible.

In the course of this chapter we have examined two assumptions said to underlie beliefs in the reality of the dead: first, that the person thought to be dead is in fact still alive, and second, that beliefs concerning the dead are the products of fantasy born of a void created by bereavement. We have seen that neither assumption need be present. But in face of this conclusion what are we to make of the assertion, 'The dead are dead'? Some philosophers want the assertion to serve as an opposition to all views about the reality of the dead which ignore or obscure elementary facts about death. But which views are these? From our discussion we can see that such views would refer only to those which involve filling a void by the imagination; only to those views which involve fantasy. Wisdom's child of faith believes that his father is still alive, but we know that his father is not alive. Norton's love for his mother was such that he wanted to be with her again. He dies thinking that all is to be restored. The tragedy of the story consists partly in the fact that these things cannot be restored, and that the father who could have restored something to the child's life only realizes this when it is too late. In examples such as these one can speak of people failing to realize, or to terms with, the fact that the dead are dead.

But many philosophical inheritors of Hume's legacy want to speak in this way of all beliefs concerning the reality of the dead. But what would be the point of insisting that the dead are dead in face of these beliefs, since that elementary fact is not denied? The various beliefs concerning the reality of the dead are themselves reactions to the deaths of human beings, various ways of understanding those deaths. There is no fantasy involved; no filling of the void by the imagination. Many philosophers, in insisting that the dead are dead in the face of *these* beliefs, would still want their insistence to be understood in the way one understands it when asserted in the face of beliefs involving fantasy. In the latter context, something is denied which the philosophers assert and want to remind us of. But in the former context, the fact of death is not denied. Therefore, when philosophers insist that the dead are dead in face of these beliefs, their insistence does not, as they think, protest against fantasy. The only function it can serve, consciously or unconsciously, is as a protest against the status accorded to the dead in the beliefs concerned: a protest against thinking of the dead in the ways Kierkegaard, Simone Weil and Winch describe. The protesters may feel that though the memories of the dead should be cherished, it would be foolish to allow such memories to intrude upon the decisions with which people are faced now in the course of their lives. Or perhaps the protesters feel that one should not tie oneself to the memories of the dead, however much they were loved when alive. The only realistic thing to do is to look for new relationships to replace those that death has destroyed. Such attitudes may stem from a general view that life is for the living, that those who are dead have had their chance and that what is important rests with the present. When others speak of the reality of the dead, or even worship the dead, those influenced by such a general view may well respond by saying, 'The dead are dead'.

Yet, if philosophers want to indulge in such responses, it has to be recognized that they are no longer simply reiterating an elementary fact. On the contrary, their response is seen to be as much a perspective on the dead as any other. In these circumstances, the man who says, 'The dead are dead and that is all there is to say about it' is confused if he takes himself to be saying something less than the man who says that the dead are transfigured, glorified or raised up. What we have seen is that he is not saying anything less, simply something different. He is not speaking independently of any perspective on the dead. He speaks from one such perspective himself.

Those influenced by Hume's legacy would have us believe that perspectives on the dead involve us in a problematic inference whereby we seek to establish the existence of a world beyond the world we know. What we have seen in this chapter is that perspectives on the dead need involve no such inference.

Yet, one could imagine a Feuerbachian objecting to these conclusions and claiming that they are premature. He might argue that in considering different perspectives on the dead, one is considering attitudes to a human subject, namely, dead people. But how does one move from such considerations to talk of a supernatural world where the love, wisdom, forgiveness, etc. which is spoken of is contrasted with human love, wisdom, and forgiveness? If these divine attributes are to be analysed in such a way that they turn out to be attitudes to human moral values, cannot the analysis be justly accused of being reductionist in spirit? It might be said that the reductionism encountered in this context is worse than the various kinds already discussed in this book. The reductionism involved in the explanations of religious belief offered by Frazer, Tylor Marett, Freud, Feuerbach and Durkheim is conscious reductionism. These writers had the specific aim of reducing religious language to a terminology which enabled one to explain it away. The analysis now under consideration, it might be said, is pernicious in that, claiming to give an account of religious belief, it unconsciously reduces the character of that belief. Religious belief escapes the logical challenge of Hume's criticisms only by being presented in a way which distorts its character.

Even if these objections are ultimately misplaced, they raise questions which we have not dealt with hitherto. These are the topic of the next chapter.

NOTES

1. John Wisdom, 'Gods', in *Philosophy and Psychoanalysis*, p. 150.
2. Simone Weil, *The Notebooks*, Vol. I, p. 29.
3. From a hitherto unpublished essay on Simone Weil by Peter Winch.
4. Winch mentions the way in which Sartre in *Being and Nothingness*, Pt. I, Chap. I, sect. 2, through his description of the café from which Pierre is absent, brings out how 'a world from which a certain person is absent is not the same as a world the description of which involves no mention of that person'.
5. This conclusion will have to be modified somewhat where the last descrip-

tion of possible relations to the dead loved one is concerned. See Chap. Nine, p. 146.

6. All extracts are taken from Flannery O'Connor, 'The Lame Shall Enter First', in *Everything That Rises Must Converge*, Faber and Faber, 1966, pp. 143–90.

7. Søren Kierkegaard, *Purity of Heart*, p. 80.

8. In other contexts it does make sense to speak of the status of the dead changing. See the use made of Bridges's poem in Ch. 9.

Nine
Unconscious Reductionism

So far in this book we have been concerned, in the main, with examples of conscious reductionism in reflections on religion by those who have been influenced, directly or indirectly, by Hume's philosophical legacy. In the last chapter, through a consideration of perspectives on the dead, I sought to question some of the assumptions involved in reductionist methodologies. Yet, the conclusions reached can be easily confused with a reductionism of another kind, namely, unconscious reductionism.

In order to see how this can come about let us remind ourselves once again of the chief characteristics of conscious reductionism. The conscious reductionist knows that religious beliefs have no reality. They are fictions, but important fictions. They are not like harmless make-believe. On the contrary, they have dominated men's lives. Therefore, it is natural to suppose, whatever gave rise to these fictions was not something trivial. As we have seen, it has been suggested that religion arose from fear and ignorance in face of mystery; that religion arose from emotional stress or social pressure. Recognizing the genesis of religious beliefs helps us to recognize the confusions involved in them. We can then reduce religion to the realities that give rise to it, realities which we can now cope with in more effective ways. The conscious reductionist's creed can thus be summed up as follows: (a) religion is a fiction; (b) we can understand its genesis; (c) religious beliefs can be restated in the language of the realities which produced them; (d) all talk of religious factors can thus be eliminated.

The contrast between the conscious and the unconscious reductionist could not be greater. The latter's aim is not anti-religious at all. On the contrary, his aim is to give an account of the logic of religious belief. But it is at this point that the matter becomes extremely complicated. The reason he is called a reductionist is precisely because of the account of religious belief that he offers. Having presented his analysis, he is accused by others of having offered a reductionist analysis of religion. He is accused of having left out of his account of religion that which cannot, in all conscience, be left out. It is in this sense that he reduces religion to something other than it is. One can see that there could not be a greater difference between the conscious and unconscious reductionist. The former claims that religion is an illusion and seeks to reduce it to its proper status. The latter wants to present an account of religious belief, believes he has given such an account, but has, in fact, reduced religion to something which lacks some of the fundamental characteristics of religious belief. It might well be argued that any attempt to analyse religious beliefs about the dead in terms of perspectives on the dead would be a case of unconscious reductionism. In fact, it might be claimed that the kind of reductionism this would exemplify would be similar to the borderline case between conscious and unconscious reductionism found in R. B. Braithwaite's 1955 Eddington lecture on 'An Empiricist's View of the Nature of Religious Belief'. These claims are confused. In bringing out the confusion involved we shall see again why the terms of Hume's philosophical legacy are inadequate for an understanding of religious belief.

Braithwaite's lecture was written very much under the shadow of logical positivism with its creed that meaningful statements could be divided into two categories: first, the propositions of logic and mathematics, and second, empirical propositions. Religious beliefs fall into neither category and so their meaning becomes problematic. If religious beliefs are assimilated to propositions of logic and mathematics, Braithwaite argued, they sacrifice all claims to have anything to do with existence. On the other hand, if religious beliefs are assimilated to empirical propositions, even allowing for the sophistication introduced into this category by the role of abstract models in science, religious beliefs would have to be falsifiable in principle. Clearly, neither alternative will do. Does this mean that religious beliefs are meaningless? At this point Braithwaite says that the positivistic criteria of meaning are too narrow and that we must heed Wittgenstein's advice and look at the way in which concepts are actually used. If we do this, we find that there is a class of concepts which does not fit into the positivistic categories, namely, moral concepts. But, Braithwaite argues, if we note how these concepts are used we see that this does not matter, since the main function of moral concepts is to express intentions to act in a certain way. Religious beliefs are best understood in this way too, but with the additional requirement that the intentions cover not only overt behaviour but the inner life as well. For religion, it is not enough that the deed is done; the spirit in which it is done is equally important. I do not think that Braithwaite's characterization of moral beliefs or of the difference between them and religious beliefs is satisfactory, but that is not our concern at the moment. More to the point is the problem that this characterization left on Braithwaite's hands. I have in mind the embarrassing wealth of material in religion concerning creation, providence, judgement, and so on. What could Braithwaite make of such language, given his view? His answer is interesting:

> Stories about the beginning of the world and of the Last Judgement as facts of past or of future history are believed by many unsophisticated Christians. But my contention is that belief in the truth of the Christian stories is not the proper criterion for deciding whether or not an assertion is a Christian one. A man is not, I think, a professing Christian unless he both proposes to live according to Christian moral principles and associates his intention with thinking of Christian stories; but he need not believe that the empirical propositions presented by the stories correspond to empirical fact.[1]

Obviously, the question facing Braithwaite is that of accounting for the relation between the religious stories and moral conduct. His reply is that the relation is a psychological and causal one. The stories simply aid a man in his moral resolutions. Braithwaite says that 'The story may pschologically support the resolution, but it does not logically justify it' (p. 89).

Such is the core of Braithwaite's argument. But is Braithwaite a conscious or unconscious reductionist? This is not an easy question to answer, since there are elements in his essay which could lead one to answer either way. He can be made to appear as a conscious reductionist in the following way: Braithwaite is in no doubt that stories about creation and a last judgement purport to be telling about empirical facts. As such, they are plainly false. We must therefore reduce the status of such stories from that of empirical propositions to that of psychological aides to moral endeavour. But Braithwaite can also be made to appear as an unconscious reductionist. He can be taken to be saying that for some religious believers, religious stories, such as those we have mentioned, are believed as though they were empirically true. In fact, not only are they not empirically true, they do not claim to be empirically true. The proper analysis of these stories is one that recognizes what their role really is, namely, that of stories or fables that act as psychological aids to moral endeavour. Here, Braithwaite would be seen, not as someone who said that religious stories are false empirical propositions, but as someone who denied that they should be characterized in this way in the first place. He then offers what he takes to be the correct characterization of the stories. In doing so, he is called a reductionist by many, albeit an unconscious one. The charge is made, rightly in my view, because in the account he does give of religious stories Braithwaite reduces the status they have in religious discourse. Of course, he himself does not realize this and would claim to be giving an account of the status that the stories do have. But it is precisely the fact that he does not see that he has reduced the status of the stories that makes him an unconscious reductionist.

My aim is not to determine how exactly Braithwaite should be interpreted. By concentrating on the reactions to his essay, however, we can see how contemporary philosophers of religion still think that their enquiries are limited by Hume's terms of reference. The fundamental confusion in Braithwaite's argument can be found in the choice with which he takes himself to be confronted. If we take the religious belief in a last judgement as our example, Braithwaite thinks that it must either be construed as an empirical proposition, such that believing in it is to predict that an event of a certain kind is going to take place some time in the future, or the story of a last judgement must be seen as a psychological aid to moral endeavour, the question of whether one believes in the truth of the story being unimportant. In reacting to these exclusive alternatives most contemporary philosophers of religion call Braithwaite a reductionist because he does not stress the first alternative. In other words, they believe that if any account of a last judgement is to be non-reductionist, we must think of it as a matter of fact, a future event. Braithwaite himself is not free from these assumptions, since when he insists that one does not have to believe in the story of a last judgement, that is, believe it to be true, this is because for the story to be true for him it *would* have to refer to a matter of fact, a future event. His analysis does not, in fact, go far enough. Because he shares the same conception of truth and falsity as the philosophers he disagrees with, he cannot call the religious stories true or false. He simply speaks of them as psychologically efficacious in supporting moral conduct. Braithwaite does not realize that in these religious beliefs, the grammar of 'belief' and 'truth' is not the same as in the case of empirical propositions or the prediction of future events.

For Braithwaite, the content of one's moral intentions is quite independent of the religious stories. The stories simply provide psychological aid for these intentions. He never considers the possibility that the religious belief is itself the expression of a moral vision. One is taught about a day of judgement, not as just one more matter of fact which is to occur in the future. One is told that it is necessary, unavoidable, something that confronts us all. One may be able to deceive one's fellow man about one's intentions and the motives of one's conduct, but at death all is revealed. The heavens may declare the glory of God, but they also declare the sins of every man. This is not a version of the belief that you will be caught out in the end. On the contrary, it gets its force from the conviction that one is known for what one is all the time—it is necessarily shouted to the heavens although one may have thought it to be the darkest secret. This is part of the idea of being alone before God, which is independent of any thought that an individual has found something out about one. The word 'God' has its sense in this context from this conviction of a necessary scrutiny by love and goodness, a scrutiny unlike that of any human agency since any idea of its being mistaken or misinformed is ruled out. An example of the religious expression of this conviction is found in the following:

O Lord, thou has searched me, and known me. Thou knowest my downsitting and mine uprising, thou understandest my thought afar off. Thou compassest my path and my lying down, and art acquainted with all my ways. For there is not a word in my tongue, but, lo, O Lord, thou knowest it altogether. Thou hast beset me behind and before, and laid thine hand upon me. Such knowledge is too wonderful for me; it is high, I cannot attain unto it. Whither shall I go from thy spirit? or whither shall I flee from thy presence? If I ascend up into heaven, thou art there: if I make my bed in hell, behold, thou art there. If I take the wings of the morning, and dwell in the uttermost parts of the sea; Even there shall thy hand lead me, and thy right hand shall hold me. If I say Surely the darkness shall cover me; even the night shall be light

about me. Yea, the darkness hideth not from thee; but the night
shineth as the day: the darkness and the light are both alike to
thee. (Psalm 139, vv. 1–12)

When this language is torn from its natural surroundings, we arrive at the philosophical discussions regarding God's omniscience and
speculations regarding whether God could know the winner of to-
morrow's 3.30! One forgets the moral vision expressed in the language of divine scrutiny. This language is not contingently related
to the believer's conduct as a psychological aid to it. On the contrary,
it is internally related to it in that it is in terms of this language that
the believer's conduct is to be understood. It is a language which in
itself gives the believer certain possibilities in which to live and
judge his life. Hence the kind of necessity connected with religious
beliefs. They are certainly not hypotheses. It is even misleading to
call them propositions. Though the term has dangers of its own, to
avoid the associations of the above terms, it would be better to call
the religious beliefs dogmas: the absolutes of faith.

For Braithwaite, believing in the last judgement means believing
that the empirical claims made by the story are true. But we have
been suggesting that belief in the last judgement does not involve
belief in a future empirical event. Neither is it a story. It is not
taught as such or believed as such. It is no more a story than morality is a story. If one thinks of the belief as an hypothesis about a
future event, does one even know how to begin to test it? One does
not know what would count here as good or bad evidence. The whole
notion of evidence seems out of place. Because language concerning
a day of judgement is in the future tense some have felt this sufficient
to establish that it refers to a future event. The conclusion is premature since there are other possibilities. If, as we have suggested,
the language of a final judgement gives men one means of reflecting
on the meaning of their lives as completed wholes, the use of the
future sense is natural enough. One's death is always a future event
for one. We have already seen in the previous chapter that talk of
a completed life is importantly different in many respects from talk
of a life which is still in progress. Belief in a final judgement is not
a *means* of expressing thoughts about a completed life, but a form
of language which makes it possible to have certain thoughts about
a completed life. This is why two men who disagree about whether
there is a final judgement are very different from two men who dis-

agree about the truth of an empirical proposition. Wittgenstein brings out the differences quite neatly when he says:

> Suppose someone were a believer and said: 'I believe in a Last Judgement', and I said: 'Well, I'm not so sure. Possibly.' You would say that there is an enormous gulf between us. If he said 'There is a German aeroplane overhead', and I said 'Possibly, I'm not so sure', you'd say we were fairly near.[2]

What, then, does belief amount to here if it is not a matter of believing in the truth of certain empirical propositions? Wittgenstein suggests that

> Here believing obviously plays much more this role: suppose we said that a certain picture might play the role of constantly admonishing me, or I always think of it. Here, an enormous difference would be between those people for whom the picture is constantly in the foreground, and the others who just didn't use it at all. (p. 56)

To believe in the last judgement is to think of admonishment in this way, to find oneself answerable in this way, to be able to say, 'Lord, thou hast searched me and known me'.

It will not do to characterize such language as a psychological aid to moral endeavour, since for those who use it and believe what it expresses, the meaning of their endeavours is given in the language. Yet, those who criticize Braithwaite's account think that matters should be rectified by reasserting the referential character of the language of religion: that the language of the last judgement refers to a future event, that the language of searching, knowing, encompassing, refers to an individual called God. Philosophy of religion has suffered from this nest of grammatical confusions. These grammatical confusions, by which I mean, in this context, mistaking one kind of language for another, are not confined to religious conceptions of eternity. Consider, for example, the way in which the same confusion could be found in an attempt to understand what has been called an eternal pact between lovers in death. An example of what I mean can be found in an elegy by Robert Bridges, where he tells of a lady who dies of grief having heard that her betrothed has been killed. At her funeral she is laid in a cedar litter on the river:

But now for many days the dewy grass
Has shown no markings of his feet at morn:
And watching she has seen no shadow pass
The moonlit walk, and heard no music borne
Upon her ear forlorn.
In vain has she looked out to greet him;
He has not come, he will not come, alas!
So let us bear her out where she must meet him.[3]

The meeting spoken of here is necessary, unavoidable, in a way
which is different in kind from any meeting between the living however well planned. This counts against Feuerbach's view that conceptions of eternity must be projections of scenes from human life.
The necessity of the meeting cannot be understood without reference
to death: it is a union of lovers in death. Such a belief becomes the
product of the kind of fantasy born of love and the need for consolation which we discussed in the last chapter, once it is thought to be
similar to a meeting in this life, the only difference being that it takes
place in another realm. This is true even when the vision of such a
union involves changes in the status of the dead which seem to
resemble changes which can occur to a human being during his life-
time. Bridges says of the lady's dead lover,

And thou, o lover, that art on the watch,
Where, on the banks of the forgetful streams,
The pale indifferent ghosts wander and snatch
The sweeter moments of their broken dreams,—
Thou, when the torchlight gleams,
When thou shalt see the slow procession,
And when thine ears the fitful music catch,
Rejoice, for thou art near to thy possession.

The lives of the lovers had been so bound up with one another that
when one is over the other becomes meaningless. What can be said
of the restless state of the lover in death is determined by the fact
that he is separated from his loved one. When she dies too, what can
be said of him in death changes accordingly. But the restlessness
depicted here has little in common with the restlessness one associates
with Borley Manor!

Now what if someone were to say, 'But the vital question is

whether what the poet says is true? Do his words refer to a true state of affairs?' Would not this reveal a massive misunderstanding? What Bridges gives us is an expression of the meaning of the deaths of the lovers. He gives us a language in which such a meaning is possible. To say that this meaning is true is to adopt it and to proclaim it. It is to say, 'This is how it is with the deaths of these lovers'. It is a grammatical confusion to think that this language is referential or descriptive. It is an expression of value. If one asks what it says, the answer is that it says itself.

When we turn from such expressions of eternal love to specifically religious conceptions of eternity, one will find a wide variety of cases. Consider, for example, the expression of eternity found in belief in Valhalla: the vision of the great banquet hall in eternity through the five hundred and forty gates of which the warriors issue daily to engage in battle, returning at nightfall to feast with Odin and the gods. Here we have a very different conception of eternity from that found in Christianity. Nevertheless, what we have here, too, are values which are fixed in a view of human destiny and which serve as mirrors in which human beings see themselves. If one reacted to this example by asking whether in fact there is going to be such a banquet, one would be repeating the kind of confusion mentioned in the discussion of the previous example.

When one turns from these two examples to the ways in which reactions to death enter Christian beliefs, one has to note important differences. In the previous examples features of human life are transformed into fixed eternal expressions of the meaning of life or of particular deaths. In Christianity, reflection on death itself creates a new attitude to all earthly things, an attitude which, in Christianity, is closely bound up with the distinction between the eternal and the temporal. For the Christian, the necessity and unavoidability of death show the essential contingency of all things, his own creature-hood, that all things are a gift, that nothing is his by right. His response to this is one of humility and gratitude. For example, he sees each new day as a gift from God. If someone were to try to understand the notion of a gift in this context, the sense in which a day can be said to be given, in terms of one person making a gift to another, the sense in which a day can be seen as given would be destroyed. The same is true of the sense in which we speak of talents being given. Some people may speak of natural gifts and not be led to worship. For others, this sense of the given leads to prayer and

L

worship. In face of what is given, the believer kneels. Talk of 'God' has its sense in this reaction. It is not the name of an individual; it does not refer to anything. No individual could give a day to men, since the sense in which a day can be said to be given depends on the absence of any such giving. The most commonly held secular counterpart to divine grace is called luck. The believer's sin is to behave in relation to people and things as if they were his by right. The Christian ideal is to see things as a gift of grace. Reflection on death is one expression of this ideal. Saint Paul connects the possibility of resurrection with dying daily. Christianity has, at its centre, a Cross—a divine self-renunciation. It is by dying to this world that the Christian finds the possibility in Christ of being glorified, transformed, raised up.

Here, briefly hinted at, one has different conceptions of eternity. But those who accuse such accounts of reductionism will want to ask what such conceptions refer to. They want to ask this sort of question: It is all very well saying that a belief in a last judgement can play a role in people's lives, but the question remains of whether in fact there is going to be a day of judgement. But our discussion of conceptions of eternity show such questions to be the product of confusion. A notion of reference is being imported into the beliefs which is quite alien to them. This can be brought out by considering Wittgenstein's remarks about the way in which the word 'God' enters people's lives:

> The word 'God' is amongst the earliest learnt—pictures and catechisms, etc. But not the same consequences as with pictures of aunts. I wasn't shown (that which the picture pictured) (p. 59).

People who ask, 'But does the picture or belief in a day of judgement refer to anything?' want to be shown that which the picture pictures. But if this could be done it would not be the same kind of picture. Wittgenstein says that he 'could show Moore the pictures of a tropical plant. There is a technique of comparison between picture and plant' (p. 63). In this case, if someone used the pictures of the plants as proof of the reality of the plants someone might say, with justification, 'I shan't be convinced if you can only show me these pictures. I shall only be convinced when I see the plants'. If, on the other hand, having heard of people praising the Creator of heaven and earth, glorifying the Father of us all, feeling answerable to the One who sees all, someone were to say, 'But these are only religious perspectives, show me what they refer to', this would be a misunderstanding of the grammar of such perspectives. The pictures of the plants refer to their objects, namely, the plants. The religious pictures give one a language in which it is possible to think about human life in a certain way. The pictures (and here one should bear in mind that 'picture' here covers related terms such as 'model' or 'map') provide the logical space within which such thoughts can have a place. When these thoughts are found in worship, the praising and the glorifying does not refer to some object called God. Rather, the expression of such praise and glory is what we call the worship of God.

Many philosophers would react to these conclusions by saying that if religious perspectives do not refer to anything, they are simply a form of disguised atheism. But this takes no account of the conceptual character of the investigation. If, *per impossible*, there were an object corresponding to these pictures or perspectives, it could not be the God of religion, any more than any actual banquet hall could be Valhalla. It seems at first as if the problem regarding God's existence is that it cannot be verified in the way one could verify the existence of antelopes, zebras or even thunder. But the problem is more acute than this, for neither will it do to say that all is well if God's existence were verifiable in this way. John Wisdom sums up the difficulty as follows:

Now what would it be like to see God? Suppose some seer were to see, imagine we all saw, move upwards from the ocean to the sky some prodigious figure which declared in dreadful tones the moral law or prophesied most truly—our fate. Would this be to see God? Wouldn't it just be a phenomenon which later we were able to explain or not able to explain, but in neither case the proof of a living God. (p. 11)

One seems to have reached a dead-end: one begins by insisting that God's existence should be verifiable, but one concludes that anything whose existence could be verified cannot be God. As we have seen in previous chapters, this paradox is one typical motive for saying that religious beliefs must be restated in ways which avoid these difficulties. Since God is in fact not seen, and since anything that is in fact seen could not be God, belief in God cannot be what it appears to be.

150 *Unconscious Reductionism*

This argument, handed down in Hume's legacy, is not, however, the only possibility. It is difficult to realize this because positivism still exercises an enormous influence over our thinking about religion. It is all too easy to conclude that if religious expressions which involve talk of God are not referring expressions, if no object corresponds to such talk, such expressions cannot say anything nor can they be held to be true. In this chapter, however, we have seen that this argument contains unwarrantable assumptions. We have argued for other possibilities. When these are recognized we see that religious expressions of praise, glory, etc. are not referring expressions. These activities are expressive in character, and what they express is called the worship of God. Is it reductionism to say that what is meant by the reality of God is to be found in certain pictures which say themselves? If we mean by reductionism an attempt to reduce the significance of religious belief to something other than it is, then reductionism consists in the attempt, however sophisticated, to say that religious pictures must refer to some object; that they must describe matters of fact. That is the real reductionism which distorts the character of religious belief.

NOTES

1. R. B. Braithwaite, 'An Empiricist's View of the Nature of Religious Belief', in *The Philosophy of Religion*, ed. B. Mitchell, p. 86.
2. Ludwig Wittgenstein, *Lectures and Conversations on Aesthetics, Psychology and Religious Belief*, p. 53.
3. Robert Bridges, 'Elegy' in *Poetical Works*, Oxford, 1912.

Ten

'Does God Exist?'

At the end of Chapter Seven we concluded that religious beliefs and practices expressed a form of language of which it made no sense to ask, 'Why do you say that?' or 'What makes you say that?' In denying the appropriateness of such questions where religious beliefs are concerned, I had in mind the various attempts at explaining religious belief which have been discussed in the course of this book. Philosophers, anthropologists, and psychoanalysts, in seeking explanations of religious belief, have often regarded such beliefs as fictions, which, in being rendered intelligible, are reduced to non-religious terms. What we have seen, however, is that in this sense of explanation, religious beliefs are irreducible. If one asks what they say, the answer we have argued for is that they say themselves. One may be interested in investigating the consequences of various religious beliefs for other social movements and institutions, or the historical development of religious beliefs. Yet, such investigations would not be an investigation into the impressiveness of the beliefs. The impressiveness may be elucidated—we have seen how symbol may be placed alongside symbol—but it cannot be explained.

Yet, having drawn these conclusions, obvious difficulties arise which need further discussion. If one says that in face of religious belief it makes little sense to ask, 'Why do you say that?' and cites as support for this conclusion the kind of language involved in the beliefs, someone might well object by saying that if the language of religious affirmation must be heeded by philosophers, so must the language of rebellion and denial in which religious beliefs are rejected. This is an important point, but the foregoing discussion of religious beliefs is not related solely to the affirmation of religious belief. To be clear about the kind of language expressed in religious beliefs is essential to an understanding of affirmation and denial in relation to religion. Yet, there are important grammatical differences between such affirmation and denial in this context and affirmation and denial in other contexts. These differences will be the concern of this chapter. The problem can be expressed as follows: In giving an account of religious beliefs one may stress the kind of necessity associated with them and say that they cannot be questioned. Immediately, however, one is faced with the undeniable fact that such beliefs *are* questioned and that this questioning is often the prelude to rejection. The task facing the philosopher is that of giving an account of the questioning of religious beliefs in a way that does not distort the kind of necessity associated with them, but also that of giving an account of this necessity in such a way that the possibility of questioning religious belief together with its possible rejection is not diminished.

This task brings us, in fact, back to the opening chapter of the book in which we mentioned the odd position of the philosophy of religion in relation to the object of its investigation. In no other branch of philosophy is it assumed so widely that the purpose of the investigation is to establish the truth or falsity of particular existential claims. For example, we do not say that philosophy establishes whether tables and chairs exist, but many do say that philosophy establishes that God does not exist. In this chapter I shall argue that philosophy neither establishes that God exists nor that He does not exist. This does not mean either that philosophy establishes agnosticism as the only appropriate response to religious claims. My point is that it is not the business of philosophy to settle such claims. It is not part of philosophy's task to establish what we can know, and hence it is not its task to establish whether we know that there is a God. Yet, all these conclusions need argument. These arguments are best brought out by a consideration of the role of the appeal to that which cannot be questioned within and outside religion.

One of the fundamental roles of the appeal to that which cannot be questioned outside religious examples can be illustrated by the dispute in contemporary philosophy concerning what have come to be known as Moore's truisms. In an article called 'A Defence of Common Sense'[1] Moore presented a list of propositions which he said he knew to be true. Among these propositions were the following: There exists a living human body which is my body. Other human beings exist. The earth has existed for many years. The mantelpiece is nearer to me than the bookcase. Yet, as Moore pointed out, when one considers the implications of what some philosophical theories have said, it seems that one would have to deny the truth of these propositions. When this occurs it is a sign that there is something wrong with the philosophical theories concerned. Norman Malcolm characterizes Moore's method as follows:

Philosopher: There are no material things.
    Moore: You are certainly wrong, for here is one hand and here is another, therefore there are at least two material things. (Proof of an External World.)
Philosopher: Time is unreal.
    Moore: If you mean no event precedes or follows another event you are wrong, for after lunch I went for a walk and after that I took a bath; and after that I had tea. (The Conception of Reality, *Philosophical Studies*, p. 210.)
Philosopher: Space is unreal.
    Moore: If you mean that nothing is ever to the right of, or to the left of, or behind, or above anything else, then you are certainly wrong; for this inkwell is to the left of this pen, and my head is above them both.
Philosopher: No one ever perceives a material thing.
    Moore: If by 'perceive' you mean 'hear', 'see', 'feel', etc., then nothing could be more false; for I now both see and feel this piece of chalk.
Philosopher: No material thing exists unperceived.
    Moore: What you say is absurd, for no one perceived my bedroom while I was asleep last night and yet it certainly did not cease to exist.[2]

Controversy has surrounded the issue of how the philosophical theories Moore is rejecting are to be understood, and how the kind of appeal to counter-instances Moore makes in rejecting them is to be understood. There is little doubt that Moore himself saw the philosophical theses as false empirical propositions. He appealed, in refuting them, to what he took to be true empirical propositions. His point would be that in accepting the philosophical theories as true one would be committed to rejecting propositions which have a greater certainty, namely, the propositions Moore appeals to in rejecting the philosopher's claims. While not denying that this is how Moore understood his own philosophical methods, Norman Malcolm has argued that this is not the best way in which Moore can be understood. If we accept Moore's own view of his work,

Malcolm argues, we shall have to say that the various philosophers whose theses he rejects were propounding false empirical propositions. But, Malcolm argues, this is absurd. 'If the philosopher's statement were an empirical statement, we can see how absurdly unreasonable it would be of him to make it' (p. 352). Malcolm is echoing a view of Wittgenstein's here once expressed in the remark, 'Those philosophers who have denied the existence of matter have not wished to deny that under my trousers I wear pants.' Moore denied this view explicitly:

> If by this Wittgenstein meant that no philosophers who have ever denied the existence of matter have ever wished to deny that pants exist, I think the statement is simply false. Some philosophers, at all events sometimes have meant to deny this: they have meant to assert that no such proposition as pants exist is true; and it was only against this assertion that I supposed my proof to be a proof.[3]

Here, it seems to me, Moore is right as against Wittgenstein and Malcolm. They argued that because what was said by the philosophers Moore opposed cannot be said, therefore the philosophers concerned could not have meant to say it. The point is that it is precisely because the philosophers concerned failed to recognize that what they wanted to say could not be said, that they said what they did. They suggested that the kind of ordinary usage of language to which Moore appealed needed revision. They denied that such a use of language was a proper use. Malcolm argued that Moore is best understood as a philosopher who reminded his fellow philosophers of ordinary usage, and denied the impropriety imputed to it. Malcolm denies that the philosophers Moore attacked were denying straightforward empirical propositions. How could they be thought of as doing anything so stupid? What is happening is that Moore is reminding them that there is an ordinary use of the forms of language which they want to reject or revise. But in criticizing Malcolm, V. C. Chappell says that this picture of the philosophers concerned is just as incredible as the one Malcolm was attacking. Malcolm says that it is incredible to think that these philosophers denied empirical statements which everyone knew to be true, but is it not equally incredible to think that these philosophers denied that there are ordinary uses of language that everyone is acquainted with? 'I do not see that Moore's philosopher is any harder to swallow than Malcolm's is.'[4]

Yet, if the dispute is left at that point, the depth of the problems worrying Moore is untouched. It seems that we must either choose between philosophers disagreeing over the truth or falsity of certain empirical propositions, or philosophers disagreeing over whether there are certain ordinary uses of language. In either case, the dispute seems uninteresting. What needs to be brought out is that although Moore was right as against Wittgenstein and Malcolm in the account he gives of what some of the philosophers he was opposing thought they were doing, he was wrong in thinking that the dispute between them can be characterized as a dispute about the truth of certain empirical propositions. What this obscures is why the philosophers Moore opposed argued in the way they did, and what the force of Moore's appeal to ordinary language amounts to. Here, Malcolm's appeal to ordinary language is important, even if it is perhaps not best expressed in the way he argues in the article we have mentioned. The point is that the metaphysical theses are based on mistakes about language and hence obscure the role of certain propositions in the language, the kind of proposition expressed in Moore's truisms.

The centrality of issues concerning language in metaphysical theses can be illustrated by some remarks by A. J. Ayer concerning empirical propositions:

> We do indeed verify many such propositions (i.e., propositions which imply the existence of material things) to an extent that makes it highly probable that they are true, but since the series of relevant tests, being infinite, can never be exhausted, this possibility can never amount to logical certainty...
>
> It must be admitted then that there is a sense in which it is true to say that we can never be sure, with regard to any proposition implying the existence of a material thing, that we are not somehow being deceived; but at the same time one may object to this statement on the ground that it is misleading. It is misleading because it suggests that the state of 'being sure' is one the attainment of which is conceivable, but unfortunately not within our power. But, in fact, the conception of such a state is self-contradictory. For in order to be sure, in this sense, that we are not being deceived, we should have to have completed an

infinite series of verifications; and it is an analytic proposition that one cannot run through all the members of an infinite series. . . Accordingly, what we should say, if we wish to avoid misunderstanding, is not that we can never be certain that any of the propositions in which we express our perceptual judgements are true, but rather that the notion of certainty does not apply to propositions of this kind. It applies to the a priori propositions of logic and mathematics, and the fact that it does not apply to them is an essential mark of distinction between them and empirical propositions.[5]

It can be seen from these remarks that Ayer is denying that an empirical proposition of the form 'I know that p' is a proper use of language. In fact, such expressions are self-contradictory. They give the impression that one has achieved what logically cannot be achieved. Of course, Ayer is right in pointing out a distinction between logical and empirical propositions. As a result of observing it, however, he wants to conclude that the notions of 'knowledge' and 'certainty' have no application where empirical propositions are concerned. But why should one assume that 'knowledge' and 'certainty' always amount to the same thing in all contexts? Why elevate one use of language and make it a paradigm for all others? According to Malcolm, Moore is best understood as someone who was asserting, in face of scepticism, that 'knowledge' and 'certainty' do have an application where empirical propositions are concerned.

But what does Ayer's argument amount to?[6] The difficulty in giving a clear answer to this question comes from the ambiguities inherent in it. These ambiguities have to do with what Ayer says about an infinite number of verificatory tests where empirical propositions are concerned. His use of 'infinite' oscillates between meaning 'so extensive as to be beyond human powers' and mathematical uses of infinity. I say this despite the fact that Ayer stresses that he is not saying that the number of verificatory tests are so great as to be beyond our powers, but that it makes no sense to speak of completing the series of tests. It is the retention of talk of completion which confuses the issue. It still suggests a large number of tests which it makes no sense to talk of completing. Yet, if we turn to mathematical notions of infinity we see that to speak of an infinite series of numbers does not refer to the extent of the series at all. It refers to the mathematical character of the series, namely, that it does not make sense to speak of the last number in the series, or that it always makes sense to ask for the next number in the series. But this does not refer to the length of the series. If Ayer were to put his point in terms which adhered strictly to mathematical conceptions of infinity, what he would be saying is that where empirical propositions are concerned, it always makes sense to say that a further verificatory test is possible or that no verificatory test one has carried out can be the final test.

Given that this is what Ayer is saying in the argument we have referred to, why should he want to say it? Part of the answer, I believe, is that because one can always formulate the contradictory of any empirical proposition, Ayer thinks that a further verificatory test could show that the contradictory of the empirical proposition one thought to be true is in fact the case. The contradictories of a logical or mathematical proposition are nonsense and have no application. Here, the certainty of the proposition is beyond any conceivable contradiction. Therefore, Ayer is led to conclude that such propositions can be said to be certain whereas empirical propositions cannot be so described.

What happens when we turn to consider actual examples? I may see food in the larder, smell it, taste it, invite others to do so, and so on. None of us entertain any doubt about these things. When I say that I am certain about these things, I mean that I do not entertain any doubt about them; that others, similarly placed and given normal senses, would reach the same conclusions, and so on. What I do *not* mean is that the statement, 'There is no food in the larder' is a self-contradiction. That does not come into consideration at all in this context. Ayer is impressed by the fact that a conception of certainty, where the contradictory of a proposition is self-contradictory, does characterize the propositions of logic and mathematics. But to point to these differences is to distinguish different areas of discourse. What is unjustifiable is the further legislative step of saying that only the uses of 'knowledge' and 'certainty' in one area of discourse shall be recognized. That it is a different use does not make it the only use. One conception of certainty is elevated and Ayer concludes that this is what we mean by certainty. In looking at actual examples we are calling Ayer back from the conception of certainty he wants to employ to the actual uses of the notion of certainty.

> When philosophers use a word—'knowledge', 'being', 'object', 'I', 'proposition', 'name',—and try to grasp the *essence* of the thing, one must always ask oneself: is the word ever actually used in this way in the language-game in which is its original home?
>
> What *we* do is to bring words back from their metaphysical to their everyday usage.[7]

When we look at this actual usage we have to ask whether it is true, where empirical propositions are concerned, that it always makes sense to seek a further verificatory test or to say that no such test can ever be regarded as final. It is in this context that Moore's truisms are of particular interest.

Commenting on these truisms in his last work, *On Certainty*, Wittgenstein thought that Moore was calling attention to some extremely important propositions. He also thought, however, that what Moore said about them was confused. Moore wanted to say of his truisms that these were things he *knew* to be true. The use of 'know' in this connection is odd. Generally speaking, when someone claims to know something one can ask him, 'How do you know?' He is committed to giving reasons which support his claim to know. Yet in relation to Moore's truisms it is difficult to see how this can be so. Any reasons offered are less certain than the claim to know something that Moore makes. For example, if one insists that one must have reasons for saying 'I know I have two hands', any reasons offered will be less certain than the proposition, 'I have two hands'. Where Moore's truisms are concerned the possibility of error seems to be ruled out. But if this is so, should one speak of 'knowledge' in connection with these truisms? One may have in mind special circumstances in which a man may wonder whether he has two hands. A man, having had one of his hands amputated, may wonder as he comes out of the anaesthetic whether he has two hands. But Moore has no such special circumstances in mind. He is thinking of ordinary situations and what he would take to be an ordinary proposition, namely, 'I know I have two hands'.

What are we to say of such propositions? Clearly, they are not propositions in logic. On the other hand, there are important differences between them and many propositions we would call empirical propositions. We may be certain about many empirical facts and yet be quite prepared to say that further investigations may make us revise our judgement. We may feel certain that a breed of animal is extinct. Nevertheless, the findings of naturalists may force us to admit that we were wrong. But can one speak in the same way about the proposition, 'I know I have two hands'? One feels like asking, 'What would it be like not to know?' and it is not clear that the question, apart from very special circumstances, has any answer. The point of asking such a question is not to underline the fact that one *does* know such things, but rather to emphasize the oddity of the use of 'know' in this context.

What would it be like to doubt whether one has two hands? Does it make sense to ask people to make sure that they have two hands? Suppose someone said that he did doubt the fact or was making sure of it. One might see him go through a series of routines, looking at his hands from all angles, checking to see if there were any mirrors present, and so on. Wittgenstein is asking whether, if anyone did all this, we would call it doubting or making sure. Surely we would not know what such a person was up to. But what lies behind our reluctance to call this doubting or making sure? Furthermore, why should this reluctance be of philosophical importance?

Wittgenstein's reply to these questions is that this reluctance has to do with the fact that talk of 'knowing', 'not knowing', or 'being mistaken' is out of place in connection with the propositions Moore was interested in. 'Showing doubt', 'being mistaken', 'making sure' only have meaning within a particular language-game. Moore said, 'There exists at present a living human body which is my body'. Would it make sense to ask Moore to make sure? Would it make sense if one had the reply, 'No, I was mistaken, there isn't an existing living body which is my body'? If someone did say this, Wittgenstein emphasized that we would *not* say that he was mistaken. We might think that he was joking or that he was mad. This is extremely important, since if a man did talk in this way it would not be a case of a mistake within a recognized way of talking, but an indication that that person had not mastered that way of talking at all. If someone has made a mistake we can advance considerations which will show that he is mistaken. If someone, on leaving a café, says, 'There does not seem to be a hat here which is my hat' he may be mistaken and we can imagine what it would be like to point out his mistake to him. But if someone says, 'There does not seem to be a body here which is my body' how does one point out his mistake to him? Pointing out a mistake is something which happens within an established procedure, whereas, in our example, that procedure cannot be taken for granted. What the person who talks in the way we have imagined stands in need of is not correction, but training. Moore, on the other hand, would respond to such a person by saying, 'What you say is false. You know that there is a living human body which is your body'. But when Wittgenstein says that 'know' is being used oddly here, he does not want to say either that 'I know that there is a living human body which is my body' or 'I do not know that there is a living human body which is my body'. He is saying that this whole way of talking is out of place here. So we must not confuse 'I know that there is a living human body which is my body' and 'I do not know that there is a living human body which is my body' where these appear to be contradictory claims with Wittgenstein's argument that 'I don't "know" that there is a living human body which is my body' and 'I don't "not know" that there is a living human body which is my body'. These latter remarks are grammatical remarks to the effect that the use of 'know' and 'not know' are ruled out in the context we are discussing. This is extremely important in directing our attention to the propositions Moore was interested in, propositions which it makes no sense to question.

Wittgenstein is interested in those things which we take for granted, things that we grow up with and never think of questioning. He does not have in mind things which, through laziness, stupidity, indifference or conformity we can't be bothered to question, but things which it makes no sense to question, except in very special circumstances where the questioning amounts to something rather different. Think of propositions like the following, 'I have a body', 'Everyone has two parents', 'If you cut off a man's limb he won't grow another one', 'The earth has existed for a long time', 'Things don't cease to exist when I am not looking for them', 'I've never been on the moon', and so on. Wittgenstein did not claim that the same could be said of all these propositions or that their status could never change. For example, On Certainty was written before the days of space travel. It is now easy to imagine circumstances where it would make sense to say, 'I doubt whether I have been on the moon'. Some critics have thought that this fact shows a shortcoming in Wittgenstein's remarks, whereas in fact it illustrates the point he is making, namely, that he is not talking of propositions which cannot be questioned because of their inherent nature. They enjoy the status they have because of the place they occupy in the language people use, a language the content of which is not independent of the complex of activities which go to make up the culture of a people. In these activities there are things we do not question, things we take for granted, and it is the propositions which are connected with such things that Wittgenstein is interested in.

We have already noted that if people are cut off from these propositions, if they do not take them for granted, they are cut of from intelligibility. We do not know what to make of them, and they do not know what to make of us. To establish an intelligible link with such people what is needed is not correction but initiation into a whole way of looking at things. This can be illustrated by our reactions to some misplaced questions by children. A child may ask us whether our house is taller than Snowdon. We do not reply by saying that in fact Snowdon is taller than our house. We would reply in such a way if the child had asked whether a cousin's house is taller than ours. But in respect of the question he did ask, what one does is to try and stop him asking it; try to get the child to stop comparing and speaking of houses and mountains in this way. One tries to initiate the child into another way of looking at the world.

What interested Wittgenstein about the propositions Moore called our attention to was that here one seems to have a number of propositions, which, in certain circumstances, and at certain times, one regards as bedrock, unquestionable. These empirical propositions become standards for testing other empirical propositions. Moore realized that these propositions had a special role, since he pointed out that if a philosopher attempted to deny them, often he was refuted by his very utterances. Moore insisted that although these basic propositions were true, they were known to be true without proof. This absence of proof interested Wittgenstein. The way in which these basic propositions hang together he called a world-picture, and he insisted that it made no sense to ask whether the world-picture was correct or incorrect, since notions of correctness and incorrectness have a meaning within a world-picture. This does not mean, however, that our norms of what is and what is not reasonable cannot change. We have already seen that such change takes place. One reason why Wittgenstein uses the term 'world-picture' is that the kind of propositions he is talking about are not based on experience. Any experience one appeals to presupposes them. When a world-picture changes this is not like the correcting of an hypothesis, as Frazer thought. When Moore said that he *knew* these propositions to be *true* he was obscuring the way they are presupposed by the things we say that we know and are true.

Yet this talk of presuppositions has its dangers. It may give the impression that these propositions which I have referred to as basic precede other empirical propositions chronologically and stand independently of them. Nothing could be further from the truth. Wittgenstein pointed out that these propositions are seldom formulated. Their reality is shown in the propositions that we do formulate. It is in this sense that they are not based on experience, but are shown in experience. For example, unless we are teaching a child, we seldom say, 'This is blue', where we mean, 'This is the colour blue'. But our taking for granted that this is blue is shown in the host of judgements we make concerning what is blue. If people did not in fact agree in their colour judgements there would be no concepts of colour. So it is misleading to say that people agree in their judgements because they presuppose agreement on what is blue, since this agreement is what is shown in their judgements.

In this connection Wittgenstein emphasizes that in mastering various language-games, the child is mastering certain activities. Concepts are acquired in *doing* certain things. When a child learns what certain objects are he learns at the same time what can and cannot be done in connection with them. When a child becomes acquainted with tables and chairs, he also becomes acquainted with the fact that he can touch them, that they are solid, that they don't disappear, and so on. That is why Moore's remark, 'This is a tree' is so artificial. A child is taught about trees and tables, not so much in a set of instructions, but in connection with a range of activities. He is not so much taught that chairs and tables exist, as to sit on a chair or put a cup on a table. What if one were to ask when the child had mastered the fact of the reality of physical objects? Isn't the answer that this is a proposition that we do not formulate? The reality of physical objects is something we show we appreciate in the way we do deal with various objects; it is swallowed down with all that. If someone suggested that the child was in doubt about all these activities we wouldn't know what to make of him. The child is taught to do certain things before it becomes acquainted with doubt and the discrimination between truth and falsity.

If we now look back at the characteristics that Wittgenstein has called our attention to in connection with these propositions Moore was interested in, we can see that they are as follows: (a) these propositions seem free from the possibility of error; (b) they are not hypotheses; (c) they are not based on experience but show themselves in experience; (d) they are rarely formulated but are involved in the ways in which we do formulate propositions in the course of our activities; (e) when people in our culture are cut off from these propositions which we take for granted and do not question, we do not say that they are mistaken, but that they must be joking or insane; (f) these propositions do not enjoy their status because of their inherent nature: changes in the culture in which we live can bring about changes in the norms of what we do and do not regard as reasonable.

At this point we must remind ourselves of our purpose in examining Moore's propositions, propositions which cannot be questioned. We did so in order to see whether the sense in which they cannot be questioned is in any way similar to the kind of necessity which seems to characterize religious beliefs. At first, it may seem that religious beliefs have very little in common with the propositions we have been discussing. Yet, on further examination, more similarities than one might have suspected become apparent. At the same time, one discovers equally important differences.

One feature we noted in connection with the propositions Moore and Wittgenstein discussed was that in connection with them one seems to have reached bedrock. We can ask why someone says that there is a tree in a garden. We may not have noticed one on a visit there. He may tell us that he was standing in front of it yesterday, telling his friend how grand it was. Normally, we should accept this as a good reason for his claim that there is a tree in the garden. But what if we asked him how he knew that there was a tree in the garden when he saw it yesterday? What would he make of this question? He might reply, 'I know a tree when I see one', but this means that he knows how to use the word 'tree'. It is odd to say that we know that there is a tree in the garden when we are standing in front of it, since there is no answer to the question, 'How do you know?' The situation is of the kind one appeals to when it *is* legitimate to ask that question. If one tries to ask the question in relation to the situation itself, one destroys the measure one employs in connection with talk of knowing, believing, conjecturing, about the existence of the tree in the garden.

Similar distinctions can be drawn where religious beliefs are

M

concerned. Here, too, one can ask, 'What reason have you for saying that your sins are forgiven?' and the reply may be that you believe this because God is merciful to sinners. But, now, is this something one can be said to know? What if the believer were asked how he knew it? He might say that he had experienced God's mercy or that God had shown His mercy in giving his Son to die for the sins of the world. Yet, what the believer has offered in reply to one's question is not evidence of God's mercy, but expressions of God's mercy. Again, a believer may say that in the Last Judgement he is eternally answerable to God. How does he know that? The usual reply one is given to these questions is that this is what the Bible teaches us and the Bible is the Word of God. The basic teaching about God—that He is a God who is merciful, loving, but also judges all men, cannot be called knowledge. In one sense these beliefs are not well established at all. If one is thinking of evidence for saying that one knows these things, there doesn't seem to be any. Wittgenstein says that the believer has 'what you might call an unshakeable belief. It will show, not by reasoning or by appeal to ordinary grounds for belief, but rather by regulating for all in his life.'[8] These beliefs are taught not as beliefs which require further reasons to justify them. They are not opinions or hypotheses. It is this feature of such beliefs which makes it odd to say that those who believe them hold opinions. 'Opinion' sounds queer in this context. Wittgenstein points out 'that different words are used: "dogma", "faith". We don't talk about hypothesis, or about high probability. Nor about knowing' (p. 57). He also shows that whereas 'belief' in connection with empirical propositions may express a degree of uncertainty, such that it makes sense to respond by saying, 'Oh, you only believe', to respond in such a way to a man who said, 'I believe in God' would be to misunderstand the use of 'believe' in this religious context.

A second feature of the propositions discussed by Moore and Wittgenstein that we noted was that if, in certain circumstances, one tried to formulate their contradictories as opposite opinions, one found that this was not possible since the 'disagreement' cannot be located within any mode of discourse. This point marked an important difference between Moore and Wittgenstein in their treatment of these questions. Moore argued as if it made sense to counter the statement, 'I do not know that I have two hands' by saying, 'Yes you do, you do know that you have two hands'. This makes it look as if the disagreement is a disagreement within our ways of talking about matters of fact. Yet, what Wittgenstein argued was that if someone was generally in the position of someone who wondered whether he had two hands, whether there was a living human body which was his body, wondered whether he was seeing a tree while standing before one, and so on, that person would not be a person with whom one disagreed about empirical matters, but someone who would not be able to master talk about such matters at all. Furthermore, if one suddenly found oneself in a position where one saw one colour when everyone else saw different colours, where one saw tables and chairs when everyone else saw an empty room, where one heard voices talking to one when no one else heard anything, one would not accuse oneself of rash judgement and resolve to be more cautious next time. On the contrary, one would suspect that one was losing one's grip on reality, that one could no longer judge or see or hear things properly. One would not be experiencing the falsification of one's views, but the collapse of those conditions which make the having of any views, true or false, possible.

Can similar conclusions be drawn about religious beliefs? To some extent they can. What we have just seen is that an attempt to contradict certain propositions leads, not to the presentation of an opposite view within a mode of discourse, but to a loss of hold on that mode of discourse. Wittgenstein raises what I believe to be a related point when he asks whether in not holding religious beliefs oneself one is contradicting the man who does hold them. He takes as an example a man who always thinks of events which happen to him as rewards or punishments. When something good happens to him he thinks in terms of a blessing and a reward from God. When he is ill he wonders what he has done to deserve the illness, or if he does something wrong he is convinced that he will be punished for it. Now, Wittgenstein asks, suppose you do not think in this way yourself at all: are you contradicting the man who does? The difficulty in replying in the affirmative is that it suggests that you are involved in the same perspective as the person who does think in terms of rewards and punishments. When I say in reply to someone who says that a public hanging is going to take place next week, 'There is no public hanging going to take place next week', I am contradicting what he says but participating in the same mode of discourse. We both mean the same by 'there will be a public hanging next week' except that one of us says that there will be such a hanging and the other denies it. My denial is within the same mode of discourse as his assertion.

This is not so, however, in the case of someone who does think in terms of rewards and punishments in the way I have described and someone who does not think in this way at all.

> If you ask me whether or not I believe in a Judgement Day, in the sense in which religious people have belief in it, I wouldn't say: 'No. I don't believe there will be such a thing.' It would seem to me utterly crazy to say this. (p. 55)

One reason why Wittgenstein says this is that the denial makes it look as if one is saying that there could be a Judgement Day, just as there could be a public hanging next week, but that as a matter of fact there won't be one. Here, one shares with the believer a belief in such things. One is only disagreeing over whether there is going to be one. Wittgenstein, on the other hand, wants to say more than this. It is not a question of his believing the opposite of what the believer thinks, but of his not sharing or having that belief at all. If one characterizes the lack of belief as believing the opposite one falsifies the character of belief and the character of non-belief. On this view, the affirmation of faith would become belief in an hypothesis or matter of fact which may or may not be the case. We have already seen, however, that religious beliefs have an absolute, necessary, character. But this view also falsifies non-belief, for it makes it look as if the non-believer shares the same mode of discourse but makes the opposite judgement within it. Whereas the non-believer does not participate in that religious mode of discourse.

> Suppose someone is ill and he says: 'This is a punishment,' and I say: 'If I'm ill, I don't think of punishment at all.' If you say: 'Do you believe the opposite?'—you can call it believing the opposite, but it is entirely different from what we would normally call believing the opposite.
>
> I think differently, in a different way. I say different things to myself. I have different pictures.
>
> It is this way: if someone said: 'Wittgenstein, you don't take illness as punishment, so what do you believe?'—I'd say: 'I don't have any thoughts of punishment'.
>
> There are, for instance, these entirely different ways of thinking first of all—which needn't be expressed by one person saying one thing, another person another thing. (p. 55)

Here, too, one finds a similarity between propositions such as 'I have two hands', 'This is a tree', 'Here is a torn page' and religious beliefs, since if one tries to contradict them one finds that one is not uttering a contradiction within a mode of discourse but cutting oneself off from a mode of discourse.

Yet, having noted two similarities between certain propositions and religious beliefs, it is equally important to note striking differences. We saw in the case of propositions like 'I have two hands', 'This is a tree', etc., that if one attempts to deny them or begins to doubt them one is cut off from reason. If I say 'There is a corridor outside my door', referring to the door of my office in which I have worked for many years, and then opening it see the sea lapping at my feet, I should say I was going mad.[9] We saw also that to have no belief in a Last Judgement is not to assert the contradictory of 'I believe in a Last Judgement', but rather to give no place in one's thoughts to that way of thinking, not to regulate one's life according to such conceptions. In this sense one could be said to be cut off from a way of thinking or from a certain perspective on life. Yet, one cannot, as in the case of the other propositions, say that the person who is cut off from religious beliefs and perspectives is cut off from reason. Partly this is because the concepts which enter into the other propositions run through a multifarious collection of activities and situations, whereas religious concepts do not. Therefore one can imagine a person having no use for the latter and still being able to share a common life with other people, whereas a person having no use for the former concepts will have cut himself off from such a life.

Another difference in this connection is what might be called the existence of alternatives in the case of religious beliefs. The point is difficult to bring out because one does not want to withdraw the view that there is nothing tentative or hypothetical about religious beliefs. Yet, because a belief makes an absolute demand on one, it does not follow that it has no alternative. All that follows is that the alternative cannot be construed as alternatives in the sense of alternative options in insurance policies, or alternative routes on a journey. The point can be brought out by a comparison between logic and morality concerning the same question. The comparison has been made as follows:

If I say, 'then the angles *must* be equal', there is no alternative; that is, 'the alternative' means nothing. If I say, 'You *ought* to want to want to behave better', there is no alternative either. The other may think, 'What if I don't?' if only because in fact he does not and there is nothing to make him. Or he may be denying what I said: it may be a way of saying, 'There is no "ought" about it'. But if he means it as a question, he has mistaken what I said: he can ask it only because he thinks I meant something else.

'You ought to make sure that the strip is firmly clamped before you start drilling.' 'What if I don't?' When I tell you what will happen if you don't, you see what I mean.

But: 'You ought to want to behave better.' 'What if I don't?' What more could I tell you?

Yet 'There is no alternative' does not mean what it does in logic. 'If the legs of the triangle are equal, the base angles *must* be equal'. Suppose my first thoughts were: 'What if I make one with the legs perfectly equal and the base angles are not equal?' You say, 'Don't talk nonsense'; or you get me to look more clearly at what I was trying to ask, and I say, 'Oh, yes'. When the man asked, 'What if I don't?' the question made no sense in that connection, although it would in others. But when I tried to ask about the logical conclusion, it was not a question at all.[10]

The comparison between 'This is a tree' and 'God created heaven and earth' has similar characteristics. In certain circumstances there is no alternative to 'This is a tree'. If the other person does not give his assent to this proposition it either means that he does not know how to use the word 'tree' or that he is cut off, unable to master our ways of talking about physical objects. 'This is not a tree' is not a genuine alternative. If these words are uttered in certain circumstances, for example, when one is standing in front of a tree, they do not express a genuine alternative, but are simply a danger signal, a sign that something has gone wrong. But one cannot say that there is no alternative to 'God created heaven and earth', since 'I don't believe it' or 'I don't accept that' expresses such alternatives. These are genuine alternatives since they indicate that the person has no use for the religious belief, that it means nothing to him, that he does not live by such a belief, or that he holds other beliefs which exclude religious faith. In this latter case, however, the alternatives are not alternatives within the same mode of discourse, but rather, different perspectives on life, some of which we have already had occasion to mention in this book.

At this point, however, many philosophers are likely to object that the argument of this chapter is needlessly complex and obscures the main issue. This is particularly true, they might argue, of the point we have just been discussing, namely, that a man who does not hold religious convictions himself may be characterized as someone who sees nothing in those convictions or as someone who holds convictions which make up a non-religious perspective. What needs to be explained, the argument continues, is the fundamental disagreement about the existence of God. Some people say there is a God and others say there is no God. This seems to involve the assertion and the denial of something or other, an object of some kind. Talk of perspectives obscures this, since the perspectives presuppose the reality of God. In this chapter there has been talk of God as merciful and as Creator of heaven and earth. But there can only be a merciful God or a God who is a creator if there is a God in the first place. It is only after we determine whether there is a God that we can proceed to determine what kind of a god He is. If one ignores this question of first importance one is in danger of being guilty of the confusions inherent in the ontological argument, namely, the confusions involved in passing from various assertions concerning the kind of being God would have to be if He existed, to the assertion of His existence. No matter how we want to talk of God's attributes, such talk does not guarantee His existence, since existence is not a further attribute.

Let us remind ourselves of the ontological argument. Anselm says that by God we mean 'a Being than which none greater can be conceived'. But then he asks whether there is such a being since

> the fool hath said in his heart, There is no God? But, at any rate this very fool, when he hears of this Being of which I speak—a being than which none greater can be conceived—understands what he hears, and what he understands is in his understanding; although he does not understand it to exist.

The argument from these premisses proceeds to the following conclusion:

> Hence even the fool is convinced that something exists in the understanding, at least, than which nothing greater can be conceived. For when he hears of this, he understands it. And

whatever is understood is in the understanding. And assuredly
that than which nothing greater can be conceived, cannot exist in
the understanding alone. For suppose it exists in the understanding
alone: then it can be conceived to exist in reality; which is greater.

Therefore, if that than which nothing greater can be conceived,
exists in the understanding alone, the very being, than which
none greater can be conceived, is one, than which a greater can be
conceived. But obviously this is impossible. Hence there is no
doubt that there exists a being, than which nothing greater can be
conceived, and it exists both in the understanding and in reality.[11]

In this argument it is clearly presupposed that existence is a
perfection and therefore a real predicate. By this I mean that Anselm
is assuming that something is more perfect if it exists than if it does
not exist. This is an extremely odd view, since if one were listing
the admirable qualities of anything, one would not include among
them the existence of the thing in question!

It makes sense and is true to say that my future house will be
a better one if it is insulated than if it is not insulated; but what
could it mean to say that it will be a better house if it exists than
if it does not? My future child will be a better man if he is honest
than if he is not: but who would understand the saying that he
will be a better man if he exists than if he does not?[12]

Malcolm shows how the question of what qualities a person has and
the question of whether a person exists are always separate questions
by asking us to

Suppose that two royal councillors, A and B, were asked to draw
up separately descriptions of the most perfect chancellor they
could conceive, and that the descriptions they produced were
identical except that A included existence in his list of attributes
of a perfect chancellor and B did not. (I do not mean that B put
non-existence on his list.) One and the same person could satisfy
both descriptions. More to the point, any person who satisfied A's
description would necessarily satisfy B's description and vice versa!
(p. 45)

Here, as Malcolm says, he is simply repeating Kant's criticisms of the ontological argument in which he pointed out that 'existence' or 'being' is not a 'real predicate':

> By whatever and by however many predicates we may think a thing—even if we completely determine it—we do not make the least addition to the thing when we further declare that this thing *is*. Otherwise, it would not be exactly the same thing that exists, but something more than we had thought in the concept; and we could not, therefore, say the exact object of my concept exists.[13]

It is not hard to see how it could be thought that the confusions inherent in the above version of the ontological argument also characterize the way I have talked about the reality of God having its meaning within certain perspectives, perspectives in which there is talk of divine mercy and a creator of heaven and earth. For, it could be said, no talk of perspectives, any more than talk of perfections, can replace enquiry into the question of whether God exists. Yet, these objections assume that what I have said about perspectives is related to the notion of God's reality in ways akin to those in which Anselm's talk of perfections was related to it. But is this so?

The first thing that has to be noted about the foregoing discussion of the ontological argument is that it involves a discussion of a being who is said to *exist*. Furthermore, the existence of this being is such that it makes sense to say that it may or may not exist. In other words, the reality of God is construed as if it were the reality of an object. I repeat: this is *assumed* in the kind of discussion of the ontological argument we have had so far. But it is precisely this assumption which needs to be examined. We have to ask whether 'the reality of God' is logically akin to the 'reality of physical objects'. This brings us back to the comparison between the kind of propositions Moore and Wittgenstein discussed and religious beliefs.

You will remember that in discussing certain propositions which play a fundamental role in our ways of talking and thinking, we mentioned the fact that these propositions are seldom formulated but show themselves in the ways we do think. For example, consider the proposition, 'Material objects exist'. The proposition is rarely formulated outside philosophy. Yet, what would it mean to deny it? It is a proposition which shows itself in the ways we do act and speak in connection with material objects. To speak of children learning that material objects exist by being taught that certain propositions are true is extremely artificial. We are reminded that

> Children do not learn that books exist, that armchairs exist, etc. etc.,—they learn to fetch books, sit in armchairs, etc. etc.
> Later, questions about the existence of things do of course arise. 'Is there such a thing as a unicorn?' and so on. But such a question is possible only because as a rule no corresponding question presents itself.[14]

We also saw that the unshakeability of these propositions does not come from their intrinsic nature, but from the role they play in a whole complex of thought and action. Making this point Wittgenstein says that

> The child learns to believe a host of things. I.e. it learns to act according to these beliefs. Bit by bit there forms a system of what is believed, and in that system some things stand unshakeably fast and some are more or less liable to shift. What stands fast does so, not because it is intrinsically obvious or convincing; it is rather held fast by what lies around it. (p. 21)

When we turn to the notion of the reality of God we find important similarities and differences. The similarity consists in the fact that the proposition 'God is real' is rarely formulated. This is even more true of the proposition 'God exists'. The latter proposition is, as we shall see, particularly misleading. But however we formulate the proposition concerning God's reality, it does not get its unshakeable character from its inherent nature, or from the kind of abstraction which philosophy tries to make of it so often, but from its surroundings, from all the activities that hold it fast. Above all, those activities involving the language of praise and worship.

Yet, once we have noted this similarity between propositions which play a fundamental role in our talk of physical objects and in people's belief in God, we have to recognize that there are also deep going differences. The surroundings that hold fast the proposition 'There are material objects' involve, as we saw, not enunciating propositions like 'Books exist', 'Armchairs exist', 'Tables exist', but certain activities such as fetching a book, sitting in an armchair, setting the table, etc., etc. In connection with these activities doubts and questions may arise. I may wonder which book you want me to get for you and you say, 'The one with the red cover.' I am then able to pick out the book you want. I may ask you which armchair is the most comfortable and you reply, 'That one'. The most comfortable armchair is picked out by pointing to it. And so on. Nothing of this sort enters into talk concerning the reality of God. There is no question here of finding out whether there is a god as I might want to find out whether there is a book on the shelf, an armchair in the room, or whether the table is set. This point has been brought out as follows:

> If one lays emphasis . . . on the fact that 'God' is a substantive, and especially if one goes on . . . to say that it is a proper name, then the natural thing will be to assume that meaning the same by 'God' is something like meaning the same by 'the sun' or meaning the same by 'Churchill'. You might even want to use some such phrase as 'stands for' the same. But nothing of that sort will do here. Questions about 'meaning the same' in connexion with the names of physical objects are connected with the kind of criteria to which we may appeal in saying that this is the same object—'that is the same planet as I saw in the south west last night', 'that is the same car that was standing here this morning'. Supposing someone said 'the word "God" stands for a different object now'. What could that mean? I know what it means to say that 'the Queen' stands for a different person now, and I know what it means to say that St. Mary's Church is not the St. Mary's Church that was here in So-and-So's day. I know the sort of thing that might be said if I were to question either of these statements. But *nothing* of that sort could be said in connexion with any question about the meaning of 'God'. It is not by having someone point and say 'That's God'. Now this is not a trivial or inessential matter. It hangs together in very important ways with what I call the grammar of the word 'God'. And it is one reason why I do not think it is helpful just to say that the word is a substantive.[15]

How then do we come to a decision about whether we mean the same by 'God'? The answer is that we do so by seeing whether worship and praise amount to the same thing for us, whether the same ideas enter into them. Within the same religion and sometimes even between religions there may be no sharp boundaries between different ideas of God. In any case it is to these contexts of religious traditions and above all, of worship, that we must turn if the idea of God's identity is to have any sense. So if someone asks *how* a person knew it was God, he could only answer in terms of what worship and praise mean to him. The question cannot be answered in the way one could answer the question, 'How do you know it was that person and not another one?' In the same article Rhees goes on to illustrate the point in the following way:

> If it was God, then it was the creator of all there is, it was that in which all things live and move and have their being. . . Nor would it be Experience of God without that. Winston Churchill may be Prime Minister and also a company director, but I might come to know him without knowing this. But I could not know God without knowing that he was the Creator and Father of all things. That would be like saying that I might come to know Churchill without knowing that he had a face, hands, body, voice or any of the attributes of a human being. (p. 131)

Talk of God's existence or reality cannot be considered as talk about the existence of an object. Neither can questions about whether we mean the same by 'God' be construed as whether we are referring to the same object. Along with this goes the recognition that the activities associated with the respective spheres concerning reality and identity will be correspondingly different. But these differences cannot be recognized unless the grammatical differences involved are recognized.

> 'God exists' is not a statement of fact. You might say also that it is not in the indicative mood. It is a confession—or expression—of faith. This is recognised in some way when people say that God's existence is 'necessary existence', as opposed to the 'contingency' of what exists as a matter of fact; and when they say that to doubt God's existence is a sin, as opposed to a mistake about the facts. (pp. 131–2)

These remarks by Rhees echo similar comments by Wittgenstein:

> If the question arises as to the existence of a god or God, it plays an entirely different role to that of the existence of any person or

object I ever heard of. One said, had to say, that one *believed* in the existence, and if I did not believe, this was regarded as something bad. Normally if I did not believe in the existence of something no one would think there was anything wrong in this.[16]

Malcolm, in his discussion of Anselm's arguments also wanted to emphasize a similar point. Having argued against Anselm's view that existence is a perfection, he calls attention to a rather different argument which he also finds in Anselm, an argument to the effect that a being who has necessary existence cannot be thought of as not existing, for to think of such a being is to see that it cannot be thought of as not existing. Malcolm sees Anselm's argument as having the force of a grammatical observation. Anselm is concerned to point out that when we talk of God we are not talking of an object which may or may not exist. Malcolm points out that it makes no sense to ask of God, 'How long has He existed?', 'Will He still exist next week?', 'He was in existence yesterday, but how about today?' (p. 49). But these questions are not senseless for the reason that God has endless duration:[17]

> According to our ordinary conception of Him, he is an eternal being. And eternity does not mean endless duration, as Spinoza noted. To ascribe eternity to something is to exclude as senseless all sentences that imply that it has duration. If a thing has duration then it would be merely a *contingent* fact, if it was a fact, that its duration was endless. The moon could have endless duration but not eternity. If something has endless duration it will *make sense* (although it will be false) to say that something will *cause* it to cease to exist. A being with endless duration is not, therefore, an absolutely unlimited being. That God is conceived to be eternal follows from the fact that He is conceived to be an absolutely unlimited being. (p. 49)

But there are difficulties in some of the conclusions Malcolm wishes to draw from his discovery of Anselm's grammatical insights. I can best bring these out by pointing to a tension between some of Malcolm's remarks. At the end of his paper he raises what he describes as the difficult question of the relation of Anselm's ontological argument to religious belief. He says that he could imagine an atheist 'becoming convinced of its validity, acutely defending it against objections, yet remaining an atheist' (p. 61). Let us pause at this admission. If the person who so reacts is an atheist then it follows that he does not believe in God. The situation is then one in which someone who does not believe in God assents to Anselm's argument. But what does this amount to? In reply to Kant's argument that when 'I think a being as the supreme reality without any defect, the question still remains whether it exists or not' (pp. 505–6), Malcolm says;

> But once one has grasped Anselm's proof of the necessary existence
> of a being greater than which cannot be conceived, no question
> remains as to whether it exists or not just as Euclid's
> demonstration of the existence of an infinity of prime numbers
> leaves no question on that issue. (p. 53)

But, as we have seen, this analogy limps. One can say that there is no alternative to Euclid's demonstration, but one cannot say that there is no alternative to Anselm's proof. Malcolm produces such an alternative at the end of his paper in his atheist who accepts and defends the proof while remaining an atheist. For such an atheist no question need remain as to whether God exists or not. But all this can mean, if the atheist has grasped Anselm's grammatical insights, is that he recognizes that in affirming one's belief in God *or in saying that one does not believe in God*, one is not talking of a being who may or may not exist. Malcolm confuses the issue when he says that 'when the concept of God is correctly understood one sees that one cannot "reject the subject". "There is no God" is seen to be a necessarily false statement' (p. 52). The point is that this only holds if 'There is no God' is construed as, 'As a matter of fact there is no God although there might have been a God'. But what Malcolm's atheist is saying cannot be so construed. All Malcolm's atheist is acknowledging is Anselm's grammatical insight. As Malcolm says, 'Surely there is a level at which one can view the argument as a piece of logic, following the deductive moves but not being touched religiously' (p. 61). Malcolm's atheist would be someone who agreed with Anselm about the kind of belief belief in God is, but cannot say himself, 'I believe in God'. It does not follow either for Malcolm's atheist, as Malcolm thinks it should, that 'The only intelligible way of rejecting Anselm's claim that God's existence is necessary is to maintain that the concept of God, as a being a greater than which cannot be conceived, is self-contradictory or nonsensical' (p. 50). Malcolm's atheist cannot confess that God's existence is necessary, since he does not believe in God. For him, talk of the necessity of God's existence is a grammatical observation about a certain kind of belief which he does not have. He may respect the belief or he may despise it, but he cannot confess it. The ambiguity is in Malcolm's description of his atheist in relation to Anselm's argument as 'becoming convinced of its validity'. This ambiguity is made possible because of a corresponding ambiguity concerning what Anselm is supposed to have achieved. On one level we can see that Anselm has thrown light on the logic of belief in God. On this view his conclusions are seen as grammatical conclusions. Anselm would be trying to clarify the character of a belief he already holds. This view finds support in Anselm's remarks in the Preface to his *Proslogion*, 'I have written the following treatise in the person of one who ... seeks to understand what he believes'. Yet when we turn to look at the conclusion of the form of the ontological argument which Malcolm finds acceptable, we find the following words, 'And this being thou art, O Lord, our God'. Of course, one could argue that here Anselm is dedicating a prior proof to God. But I do not think Anselm would have been altogether happy with that suggestion. He seems to claim that if anyone grasps his proof, he too should be able to say, 'And this being thou art, O Lord, our God'. Yet, Malcolm's atheist grasps the proof and cannot say these words. Malcolm argues that the fool of the psalm can no longer say in his heart 'There is no God' although he still does not believe in God. Malcolm says that 'It is hardly to be expected that a demonstrative argument should, in addition, produce in him a living faith' (p. 61). But, again, this simply illustrates the ambiguity in Malcolm's position. The whole issue turns on the question of who is supposed to be saying 'There is a God' or 'There is no God'. In so far as these words come from the mouths of philosophers discussing the logical status of belief in God, the most that Anselm's argument can show is that both statements about God are confused if the notion of existence involved is contingent existence. The same confusions exist in these remarks, given the above assumption, whether they be expressed by believers or atheists respectively. But what Anselm seeks to show and cannot show is that 'And this being thou art, O Lord, our God' can be the result of a demonstrative proof such that 'I do not believe in God' is ruled out as a possible response. We have seen that both the affirmative and negative responses can be uttered without implying any of the confusions which Malcolm rightly exposes. These responses cannot be the product of a proof since the affirmation and denial of faith do not have their force from such a context. Malcolm recognizes this to a great extent when he says:

> ... even if one allows that Anselm's phrase may be free of self-contradiction, one wants to know how it can have any *meaning* for anyone. Why is it that human beings have even *formed* the concept of an infinite being, a being greater than which cannot be conceived? This is a legitimate and important question. I am sure there cannot be a deep understanding of that concept without an understanding of the phenomena of human life that give rise to it. (p. 60)

The only misgiving I have about these remarks is that Malcolm seems to separate the question of whether the notion of God's necessary existence is free from self-contradiction from the question of how it can have meaning for anyone. I cannot see how one can answer the first question until one has investigated the second. We have seen the dangers in asking how religious concepts came to be formed, since such questions have led again and again to the kind of reductionist accounts of religious belief we have considered in this book. But Malcolm is surely right in linking this question to the contexts in which religious beliefs have their meaning. Referring to one such context he approves of Kierkegaard's view that

> There is only one proof of the truth of Christianity and that, quite rightly, is from the emotions, when the dread of sin and a heavy conscience torture a man into crossing the narrow line between despair bordering upon madness—and Christendom.

The trouble is, however, that Anselm's proof is not from the emotions. Malcolm says of the concept of God's necessary existence:

> When we encounter this concept as a problem in philosophy, we do not consider the human phenomena that lie behind it. It is not surprising that many philosophers believe that the idea of a necessary being is an arbitrary and absurd construction. (p. 61)

When Anselm came to consider the concept he had a living faith as a background to his investigations. Thus he was able to give us a grammatical insight into the nature of this concept. This grammatical insight can be shared by believers, atheists, or others who may not want to describe themselves in either of these ways. Yet Anselm wanted to go further. He wanted, by means of his proof, to end with the recognition, 'And this being thou art, O Lord, our God'. He wanted his proof to end in praise, to issue in an affirmation of faith, such that all denials of these truths are ruled out. Here, Anselm was confused, since he abstracted the affirmation from the very contexts which could give birth to it, so introducing the kind of ambiguity into his arguments which we have also found in Malcolm's discussions of them. There is a mixture of what must essentially be kept apart; a mixture of philosophical grammatical observations and affirmations of faith.

What are the surroundings which can lead to the affirmation, 'Thou art God'? O. K. Bouwsma argues that these surroundings are precisely those that Anselm distorted in his devising of the phrase, 'We believe that thou art a being than which none greater can be conceived', a phrase which arises 'out of a distorted reading of the words of praise'.[18] This praise is at its most forceful in the psalms. Bouwsma comments:

> And what praise it is! Compared to their praise, all other praise is tepid. Here the spirit rejoices. What jubilation and ecstasy! I know of nothing today rivaling this in intensity, that exuberance of the spirit, that extolling of what is high. Here we sing, we praise, we are glad, we bless, we magnify, we exult, we extol, we make a noise, we raise our hands, we dance, we sound the trumpet, we play on the psaltery and harp and with cymbals and dance, with stringed instruments and wind, and organs, and upon the loud cymbals and the high sounding cymbals. What were Bach and Handel doing but praising God?
>
> And now I should like to review some of the language of praise. I have chosen these particular instances as reminders we need in order that we may discover the surroundings of the phrase 'the being than which none greater can be conceived'. Here are a few:
>
> King Solomon to King Hiram: 'And the house which I build is great; for great is our God above all gods'.

N

And here is King David: 'Wherefore *thou art great*, O Jehovah God; for there is none like thee, neither is there any God besides thee, according to all that we have heard with our ears'. Compare this and the foregoing with Anselm's 'Thou art a being than which none greater can be conceived'. Anselm gilding the praise of King David.

And here are some sentences from the psalms:
Great is Jehovah and *greatly* to be praised. . . (Ps. 48)
Jehovah reigneth; let the people tremble.
He sitteth above the cherubim;
Let the earth be moved.
Jehovah is great in Zion (Ps. 99)
Bless Jehovah, O my soul.
O Jehovah, my God, *thou art very great*. (Ps. 104)
Great is Jehovah and *greatly* to be praised.
And his *greatness* is unsearchable. (Ps. 145) (pp. 258–9)

Bouwsma points out that in sentences like 'It is a good thing to give thanks unto the Lord and to sing praises unto thy name, O most high' (Ps. 92:1) and in phrases like 'too wonderful for me' the word 'high' and the superlative are being used in the same sense as 'great'. It is clear from these examples that Anselm's phrase has been torn from the context of faith and presented in the context of proof. Here, it is misleadingly presented as a statement in the indicative form. Bouwsma makes the same observation as one we noted earlier when Rhees said that '"God exists" is not a statement of fact. You might say also that it is not in the indicative mood.'[19] He asks what happens to expressions of praise like those we have considered and others like, 'O, let the nations be glad and sing for joy' (Ps. 67: 6) and 'Let the Lord be magnified' (Ps. 35: 2) when they are torn from their natural setting. He gives the following reply to his own questions:

The earlier set of sentences have the form of indicatives—'Great is Jehovah', etc. When removed from their surroundings and cooled for purposes of proof, they may be mistaken for sentences about God, as though they furnished information or descriptions. But they are no more statements or descriptions than the sentences just quoted. Those by their imperative form prevent at least that misunderstanding. The sentence, 'Great is our God above all other gods' is not to be mistaken for such a sentence as, 'High is the

Empire State Building above all buildings in New York'. Or is it? I'm afraid so. (p. 261)

By showing how 'God' has its meaning in the language of praise and worship, Bouwsma, like others we have mentioned in this chapter, wants to draw us away from the misleading talk which makes 'God' stand for an object and suggests that one could find out by some kind of an investigation whether he exists or not. If a person believes in God this is something which shows itself in his praise and worship. 'I believe in God' is, above all, an expression of faith.

To ask whether God exists is not to ask a theoretical question. If it is to mean anything at all, it is to wonder about praising and praying; it is to wonder whether there is anything in all that. This is why philosophy cannot answer the question 'Does God exist?' with either an affirmative or a negative reply. For from whose mouth does the question come and how is it answered? Praising, thanking, confessing, asking, and adoring before God may have meant little to a man. Suddenly, it means everything to him. He says that God has become a reality in his life. Has this come about by his discovering an object? Hardly. What has happened is that he has found God *in* a praise, a thanksgiving, a confessing and an asking which were not his before.[20] And if coming to God is not coming to see that an object one thought did not exist does in fact exist, neither is losing faith in God coming to see that an object one thought existed does not in fact exist. 'There is a God', though it appears to be in the indicative mood, is an expression of faith. One of its most characteristic forms is showing forth praise. 'There is no God' also appears to be in the indicative mood. But it is in fact a denial; it may indicate one of a number of possible negative relations in which a man may stand to the affirmation of faith.

The task of philosophy is to comment on the character of such affirmations and denials. Such philosophical comment may in fact clear the way or bar the way towards affirmation or denial for a person, but that is a consequence and not the purpose of the comment. In this chapter what we have done is to comment on the deep-going assumptions often involved in a philosopher's asking, 'Does God exist?' The worst misunderstanding is to think that this question is a theoretical one. Not far behind is the belief that philosophers should be able to answer it.

NOTES

1. G. E. Moore, 'A Defence of Common Sense', in *Contemporary British Philosophy*, 2nd Series.
2. Norman Malcolm, 'Moore and Ordinary Language', in *The Philosophy of George Edward Moore*, edited by Schilpp.
3. G. E. Moore, 'A Reply To My Critics', in *The Philosophy of George Edward Moore*, p. 670.
4. V. C. Chappell, 'Malcolm On Moore', p. 424.
5. A. J. Ayer, *The Foundations of Empirical Knowledge*, pp. 44–5.
6. I am not suggesting that Ayer would still advance this argument.
7. Ludwig Wittgenstein, *Philosophical Investigations*, I, 116.
8. Ludwig Wittgenstein, *Lectures and Conversations on Aesthetics, Psychology and Religious Belief*, p. 54.
9. I owe this example to Rush Rhees.
10. Rush Rhees, 'Some Developments in Wittgenstein's View of Ethics', in *Discussions of Wittgenstein*, pp. 95–6.
11. Anselm, *Proslogium*, pp. 7–8.
12. Norman Malcolm, 'Anselm's Ontological Arguments', in *Religion and Understanding*, p. 46.
13. Kant, *The Critique of Pure Reason*, p. 505.
14. Ludwig Wittgenstein, *On Certainty*, p. 62.
15. Rush Rhees, 'Religion and Language', in *Without Answers*, pp. 127–8.
16. Ludwig Wittgenstein, *Lectures and Conversations on Aesthetics, Psychology and Religious Belief*, p. 59.
17. This and the following quotation from Malcolm does not raise the question of whether the notion of endless duration is itself intelligible. There is good reason to doubt whether it is. This is a major obstacle for those who would understand God's eternity as endless duration. See R. F. Holland, 'For Ever?', *Philosophical Quarterly*, January 1974.
18. O. K. Bouwsma, 'Anselm's Argument', in *The Nature of Philosophical Inquiry*, ed. Bobik, p. 257.
19. See p. 174.
20. I have tried to show something of what is involved in such thanking, confessing and asking in *The Concept of Prayer*.

Eleven

Religion, Understanding and Philosophical Method

In the course of his discussions on the notion of belief as it appears in religious contexts, Wittgenstein, as we have seen, wanted to deny that the non-believer contradicted the believer when he said, 'I do not believe in God' or 'There is no God'. One of his reasons for this conclusion was that he did not think that 'There is a God' and 'There is no God' are contradictory statements within the same mode of discourse. They are not akin to 'There are unicorns' and 'There are no unicorns' in this respect. To say, 'There is no God' is more like rejecting a whole mode of discourse than expressing an opposite view within one. In saying this, however, further questions arise as to whether, if a whole mode of discourse is said to be rejected, a person can be said to understand what he rejects. Immediately after saying that if a man does not believe in a Last Judgement this need not be construed as the opposite of the belief when it is held, Wittgenstein raises the problem of understanding in this context.

> In one sense I understand all he says—the English words 'God', 'separate', etc. I understand. I could say: 'I don't believe in this,' and this would be true, meaning I haven't got these thoughts or anything that hangs together with them. But not that I could contradict the thing.
>   You might say: 'Well, if you can't contradict him, that means you don't understand him. If you did understand him then you might.' That again is Greek to me. My normal technique of language leaves me. I don't know whether to say they understand one another or not.[1]

Part of the difficulty comes from the fact there are a number of different levels at which one can speak of understanding religious belief. Although philosophical misunderstandings of religious belief are often, as elsewhere, misunderstandings about language, about what it means to say something to God or about God or to ask whether someone worships the same God as another person, the appeal to language has additional difficulties where religious belief is concerned. This point is emphasized by O. K. Bouwsma when he compares and contrasts the appeals made to language by Kierkegaard and Wittgenstein:

> The task in both cases is conceived as that of dispelling illusions. The illusion is in both cases one of misunderstanding certain languages. Here I see that I must be careful. Both those who seek to understand ordinary language, and those who seek to understand the scriptures run into confusion due to mistaken expectations concerning what the language must mean. Let me get this straight. In the work of Wittgenstein there is ordinary language we understand. That ordinary language is related to words or expressions that give us trouble. In ordinary language we discover the corrective of the language which expresses the confusion. In the work of Kierkegaard there corresponds to ordinary language in Wittgenstein the language of scriptures, which Kierkegaard understands. Without this latter assumption Kierkegaard cannot be effective. And this is not how it is in Wittgenstein.[2] There ordinary language is taken to be language which we all understand. Here there is agreement. But Kierkegaard's task is in that way more formidable. He has first to teach us the language of scripture.[3]

When religious beliefs are torn from their scriptural contexts they become statements of fact, theories, hypotheses, metaphysical theses. This can be illustrated by reference to Anselm's fool, since Anselm's fool is not the fool of the psalm from which he is torn.

Anselm's fool says in his heart, 'There is no God'. His mistake is that he classified 'God' among those things which do not exist, whereas he should have classified Him among those things which do exist. We have already noted the confusions involved in such a view. But these confusions could have been avoided if Anselm had remembered the sense in which the fool in the psalm had said in his heart, 'There is no God'. Bouwsma argues, correctly in my view, that the fool in the psalm is not a theoretical speculator. He is depicted as the unrighteous man:

> And when the psalmist writes that 'the fool hath said in his heart'

this is not to be understood as meaning that the fool said this to
himself, nor that when he is asked what he has said in his heart
that this would mean anything to him or that he could tell. It is
the speaking of his misdeeds which is the saying in his heart. He
utters misdeeds and they are speeches out of the fullness or the
emptiness of his heart. Actions speak neither Hebrew nor English.
There is a version here of, 'By their fruits ye shall know them'.
So the fool's deeds show, not that he is saying to himself 'There
is no God' but that he does not believe, that he neither keeps
God's commandments, nor fears God.

The psalm begins with the line already quoted. 'The fool hath
said . . . ' But it goes on, 'They are corrupt, they have done
abominable works, there is none that doeth good' and it continues,
'They are all gone aside, they are altogether become filthy,' they
'eat up my people as they eat bread.' I am emphasising this detail
in order to point out another instance of Anselm's lifting out of its
surroundings a sentence which in these surroundings has a use
which is quite different from that to which Anselm now adapts
it. . . Anselm's fool is a literate fool, but he is not the fool of this
psalm.[4]

Yet, having said this, Bouwsma shows us that there are other possibilities. Anselm tells us nothing about his fool, but we can supply
some contexts of our own. I want to quote in some detail one of the
contexts Bouwsma supplies for us since I believe it is absolutely central to a discussion of the kinds of understanding which may remain
hidden under the general phrase, 'understanding religious belief'.

Bouwsma asks us to imagine that the fool is a renegade Jew at the
time of the Captivity. He is embittered by what he sees around him.
But there is still a congregation in the town who meet each Sabbath
day. But what of the fool?

Sometimes he stands at the door where they meet and he listens
to the reading, those stirring and terrible chapters from Exodus
and Deuteronomy and he hears the injunction, 'Only take heed to
thyself, and keep thy soul diligently, lest thou forget the things
which thine eyes have seen and lest they depart from thy heart
all the days of thy life; teach them to thy sons and thy sons' sons.'
And he hears again of 'the mountain that burned with fire' and
of 'the darkness, clouds, and thick darkness' and of 'his voice out

of the midst of the fire.' He is distressed, both sad and angry. He
has neither sons nor sons' sons, and if he did what would he teach
them? He no longer believes. He is desolate, tender with memories
but without hope. God, too, is only a memory. And when he hears
the psalm, 'Bless the Lord, O my soul, and all that is within me
bless his holy name. Bless the Lord, O my soul, and forget not all
his benefits,' he stands grim at the door, looking in upon those old
men in their little black caps. But he does not enter. He turns and
walks hurriedly away. (p. 272)

Does the person depicted here understand the faith he is rejecting?
Isn't it this kind of context which leads us to say with Wittgenstein
that we do not know whether to say that he understands or not? But
what contributes to our anxiety? Why not say that he understands
exactly what the worshippers understand? Our reluctance to say this
is bound up with the fact that for them, their understanding is in-
separable from their worship. But the person at the door does not
worship. He does not do what they do. Bouwsma reminds us that
'They remember what God has done; they receive and obey the
commands as God's commands; they heed and fear God; they praise
God and they pray; they also bring their offerings' (p. 273). But the
person at the door does none of these things. In that sense he does
not possess the understanding which comes from worship. A similar
example can be found in the case of love. A person may hear love
stories, hear them being discussed and debated, etc. But if he has
never been in love, never experienced its trials, tests and tribulations,
never known its joys and exultations, then the understanding of one's
life in terms of love which can only come through such things is not
his. The same is true of faith in God. It is because this is so that many
writers have wanted to say that what 'There is a God' amounts to is
'Thou art God' and that to know God is to love Him. And when
they are concerned with the understanding that worship brings what
they say is illuminatingly correct.

   Yet, their observation cannot stand in that form if it is meant to
account for any kind of belief in God. This is because the class of
believers is wider than the class of worshippers. Bouwsma's fool
who stands at the door no longer believes. God is only a memory
to him. Yet Bouwsma tells us that he knew well enough how the
old men received the words of scripture and what they meant to
them.

But when they invited him to join them in remembering, in prayer, in praise, he shook his head and would not, could not. God to heed, to obey, to fear, to remember, to hearken to! What is God? 'A shout in the street.' And he turned away, miserable, guilty, numb. (p. 273)

There seems to be a very thin line between Bouwsma's atheist and another one could imagine at the door, longing to enter, and yet, out of fear of what he has to give up, turning away in the end. He does not call himself an atheist, for who does he long for if not for God? Another cannot be found lurking at the door at all. He hurries by without so much as a glance in that direction. And yet in the seclusion of his room and of his heart he too hears the words bidding him to hearken and obey. He does not call himself an atheist either, for whom is he fleeing from if not from God? Yet another may come to the door, but not to listen quietly but to interrupt and shake the fist. He too knows the words of scripture and hates them. He does not call himself an atheist for whom is he rebelling against if not against God? What these examples show us is that there is no sharp line between belief and unbelief. Furthermore, we cannot assume that the thoughts of the outcast have never invaded those old men in the little black caps who make up the congregation of the faithful. Indeed, in so far as any serious faith involves a strugggle to believe or the facing of various trials, one can be sure that such thoughts have certainly come their way. The various relations to God I have described illustrate the following remarks by Norman Malcolm:

I am suggesting that *belief-in* has a wider meaning when God is the object of it than when a human being is. Belief in God encompasses not only trust but also awe, dread, dismay, resentment, and perhaps even hatred. Belief in God will involve some affective state or attitude, having God as its object, and those attitudes could vary from reverential love to rebellious rejection.[5]

All the cases I have outlined have an understanding of the words of scripture, but it is not the kind of understanding which comes from worship. If one asks what kind of understanding it is, one can only reply that it is the understanding which comes from a fusion of an appreciation of the kind of claim the scriptures make on one and one's reaction of longing, fear, or rebellion as the case may be.

o

I said that there may be a thin line between Bouwsma's atheist and some of the cases I have mentioned. I should have thought that an atheist for whom the religious language of his youth had become a memory was further removed from these cases. Bouwsma says that the language of the scriptures had become a memory for his fool. The difficulty for me is that he describes his going away as miserable, guilty and numb. The atheist I am thinking of may savour the language which once regulated his life, but it is a matter of enjoying its beauty and form. Listening to the chanting choirs is, for him, like going to a concert. Further removed again is the atheist who has never had occasion to use the language of religion. In his life, religion has always been something other people did. It means nothing to him. When someone asks him whether he believes in a Last Judgement he replies, 'I don't have such thoughts', meaning not, 'I see the kind of belief you are talking about, but it does not regulate my life', but, 'Such thoughts mean nothing to me'. But the person who replies in the former way may also call himself an atheist.

It is important to note that none of the forms of atheism I have hinted at can be accused of philosophical confusion. Neither can this accusation be made of the religious beliefs which the atheist rejects. What is confused on both sides is treating 'There is a God' and 'There is no God' as statements of fact, as conclusions which result from some kind of finding out. It is also confused to think that the issues between religious belief and atheism can be settled by some kind of philosophical demonstration. Thus we saw at the opening of the book the kind of philosophical confusion one can be led into by the argument from design and the cosmological argument. But this kind of theism is itself a kind of philosophical theory which expounds certain metaphysical views. The rejection of the conclusions of such arguments can be supported by believers and non-believers alike since the criticism is essentially philosophical criticism. What such criticism amounts to is not the postulation of the opposite opinion, namely, 'There is no designer of nature' or 'There is no cause of everything', but the revealing of the confusion involved in certain theistic arguments. Those who support such arguments want to say something which cannot be said. But the atheist may want to do more than this. He may want to say that all forms of religious belief are riddled with confusions. In the course of this book some of these criticisms of religious beliefs have been considered. It has been suggested that religious belief is the product of a primitive mentality, of emotional stress, of unconscious desires or of social pressure. We have seen that these criticisms, while they may reflect certain instances of religious belief, are themselves the products of confusion in so far as they claim to give an account of religious belief in general. Theoretical atheism is rejected along with theoretical theism, both of which are attempts at philosophizing which will not stand up to examination. Yet, we have also seen that there are forms of religious belief and atheism which are independent of the metaphysical assumptions we have been criticizing. As far as philosophy is concerned, no endorsement or criticism can be made of these forms of belief and unbelief.

Even so, questions can be raised about the kind of understanding a philosopher must possess in order to fulfil his descriptive task. Clearly, if a philosopher is the kind of atheist for whom religious belief is meaningless, he will not be able to give an account of the nature of religious belief. But the same may be true of a philosopher who is a believer and who does not understand atheism. Similarly, the philosopher will fail in his task if the only religious belief and atheism he can understand is theoretical theism and theoretical atheism. We have seen, however, that there is a vast variety of different states and attitudes within the category of religious believers, since not all believers are worshippers. A person holding any of these may see the kind of thing atheism is and still reject it. Similarly, a man may see the kind of thing religious belief is and still call himself an atheist because he does not live by such beliefs—which is what 'believing' comes to in this context. The philosopher who wants to show what kind of belief religious belief is, or what kind of attitude atheism is, may have any of these attitudes or beliefs and still fulfil his task. Indeed, he may not want to describe himself in any of these ways. He may be able to share Anselm's grammatical insights, for example, without calling himself a believer or an atheist. What he must have is respect for the belief he is investigating. He may want to oppose it, proclaim it or simply note it as a serious point of view, but he cannot dismiss it as a product of confusion. This is true whether he is giving an account of religious belief or of atheism.

On the other hand, it cannot be denied that philosophical clarifications may open up or bar the way to religious belief or atheism for a person. This is because what was barred or kept open previously did rest on philosophical confusion. These results are unpredictable, and, as we have said, they are not the business of philosophy. But if the religious belief or the atheism has not been contaminated by the varieties of philosophical confusion we have met in our discussions, then in giving an account of them by making explicit the logic or the grammar of such beliefs, philosophy neither adds anything to them nor takes anything away from them. It certainly cannot provide an answer solely by its own efforts for the person who is perplexed about what he ought to believe. At best the help it may offer is indirect. But as far as the character of religious belief or atheism is concerned, philosophy leaves everything where it is. To see why this should be so, however, is itself to have arrived at an important philosophical conclusion. It is a conclusion which cuts across philosophical debates between theoretical theists and theoretical atheists. It is a conclusion which brings to light the irony of contemporary philosophy of religion where, to a large extent, philosophers sympathetic and unsympathetic to religion share the same confused assumptions that 'There is a God' is a statement in the indicative mood, and that 'God will judge us all' is a prediction of a future matter of fact. The unsympathetic to religion offer arguments to establish the falsity or unintelligibility of religious beliefs without questioning these assumptions. Some go further and attempt to show the real meaning of religious belief by exploring its genesis. Those sympathetic to religion try to meet these objections within the same terms of reference offered by the critics, unaware that in doing so they too are guilty of reductionism in their account of religious belief.

The argument of this book has been that both sides of the above dispute are equally confused. The common confusion leads the disputants to expect the way out of their puzzles to be through one of two doors, both of which being, at the moment, closed: theoretical theism or theoretical atheism. Such expectations cannot be fulfilled since these doors lead nowhere. What is needed is a change of direction, a radical turnabout, since there is a door which has been open all the time. What we need to understand religious belief or atheism are not more facts, but an appreciation of the character of what already lies before us. This book has aimed at such understanding by assembling reminders of what already lies before us. It has been faced with the additional difficulty that not all people share the languages of religious belief. Yet, despite the difficulty, philosophical enquiry, by the aid of such reminders, should at least put an end to much idle speculation carried on in the name of the philosophy of religion.

NOTES

1. Ludwig Wittgenstein, *Lectures and Conversations on Aesthetics, Psychology and Religious Belief*, p. 55.
2. This is not strictly true. Bouwsma has certain aspects of Wittgenstein's work in mind. If one thinks of *Lectures and Conversations* or 'Remarks on Frazer's *Golden Bough*' ', the same distinction could not be maintained.
3. O. K. Bouwsma, 'Notes on "The Monstrous Illusion" ', p. 12.
4. O. K. Bouwsma, 'Anselm's Argument' in *The Nature of Philosophical Inquiry*, ed. Bobik, pp. 270–1.
5. Norman Malcolm, 'Is it a Religious Belief that "God Exists"?', in *Faith and the Philosophers*, ed. Hick, pp. 106–7.

Bibliography

A. BOOKS

Anscombe, G. E. M. and Geach, Peter: *Three Philosophers*, Blackwell, 1961.

Anselm, St.: *Proslogium*, trans. S. N. Beans, Open Court, 1962.

Aquinas, St. Thomas: *Summa Theologica*, Burns and Oates, Vols. I–III, 1947–8.

Ayer, A. J.: *The Foundations of Empirical Knowledge*, Macmillan, 1940.

Blanshard, Brand: *Reason and Goodness*, Allen and Unwin, 1961.

Cassirer, Ernst: The *Myth of the State*, Yale University Press, 1961.

Drury, M. O'C.: *The Danger of Words*, Routledge, 1973.

Durkheim, Emile: *Elementary Forms of the Religious Life*, Allen and Unwin, 1915.

Evans-Pritchard, E. E.: *Theories of Primitive Religion*, Oxford, 1965.

Feuerbach, Ludwig: *The Essence of Christianity*, trans. George Eliot, Harper Torchbooks, 1957.

Fingarette, Herbert: *The Self in Transformation*, Harper Torchbooks, 1963.

Frazer, James: *The Golden Bough*, abridged ed. Macmillan, 1922.

Freud, Sigmund: *Totem and Taboo*, Routledge, 1960.

——*The Future of an Illusion*, Hogarth Press, 1962.

——Collected Papers, Vol. II, Hogarth Press, 1956.

Hepburn, Ronald: *Christianity and Paradox*, Watts, 1958.

Hume, David: *Enquiry Concerning Human Understanding*, ed. L. A. Selby-Bigge, Oxford, 1957.

——*Dialogues Concerning Natural Religion*, ed. N. Kemp-Smith, Bobbs-Merrill.

——*Natural History of Religion*, Library of Modern Religious Thought, Black, 1956.

Huxley, Aldous: *Do What You Will*, Windus, 1931.

Kamenka, Eugene: *The Philosophy of Ludwig Feuerbach*, Routledge, 1970.

Kant, Immanuel: *The Critique of Pure Reason*, trans. N. Kemp-Smith, London, 1929.

Kierkegaard, Søren: *The Journals*, trans. A. Dru, Oxford, 1938.

——*Purity of Heart*, trans. D. Steere, Fontana, 1961.

Malcolm, Norman: *Knowledge and Certainty*, Prentice-Hall, 1963.

Malinowski, Bronislaw: *Science, Religion and Reality*, ed. J. A. Needham, 1925.

Marett, R. R.: *The Threshold of Religion*, Methuen, 1914.

O'Connor, Flannery: 'The Lame Shall Enter First', in *Everything That Rises Must Converge*, Faber and Faber, 1965.

Phillips, D. Z.: *The Concept of Prayer*, Routledge, 1965.

——*Death and Immortality*, Macmillan, 1970.

Schopenhauer, Arthur: *The World as Will and Idea*, Routledge, 1957.

Tylor, E. B.: *Primitive Religion*, London, 1920.

Weil, Simone, *The Notebooks*, Routledge, 1956.

Winch, Peter: *The Idea of a Social Science*, Routledge, 1958.

Wittgenstein, Ludwig: *Philosophical Investigations*, trans. G. E. M. Anscombe, Blackwell, 1953.

——*Lectures and Conversations on Aesthetics, Psychology and Religious Belief*, ed. C. Barrett, Blackwell, 1966.

——*On Certainty*, trans, D. Paul and G. E. M. Anscombe, Blackwell, 1969.

B. PAPERS

Anderson, John: 'Freudianism and Society', in *Studies in Empirical Philosophy*, Angus and Robertson, 1962.

Bouwsma, O. K.: 'Anselm's Argument', in *The Nature of Philosophical Inquiry*, ed. J. Bobik, University of Notre Dame Press, 1970.

——'Notes on "The Monstrous Illusion"', in *The Perkins School of Theology Journal*, Vol. XXIV, Spring 1971.

Braithwaite, R. B.: 'An Empiricist's view of the Nature of Religious Belief', C.U.P., 1955, reprinted in *The Philosophy of Religion*, ed. B. Mitchell, Oxford, 1971.

Chappell, V. C.: 'Malcolm on Moore', *Mind*, Vol. LXX, 1961.

Cioffi, Frank: 'Wittgenstein's Freud', in *Studies in the Philosophy of Wittgenstein*, ed. Peter Winch, Routledge, 1969.

Drury, M. O'C.: 'Madness and Religion', in *The Danger of Words*, Routledge, 1973.

Editorial Review, 'Sociology out of its Place', in *The Human World*, No. 3, May 1971.

Freud, Sigmund: 'Obsessive Acts and Religious Practices', in *Collected Papers*, Vol. II, The Hogarth Press, 1956.

Holland, R. F.: 'For Ever?', *The Philosophical Quarterly*, Vol. 24, No. 94. January 1974.

Jones, Ernest: Obituary Article on Freud, in *International Journal of Psychoanalysis*, Vol. XXI.

Malcolm, Norman: 'Moore and Ordinary Language', in *The Philosophy of George Edward Moore*, ed. Schlipp, Evanston, 1942.

——'Anselm's Ontological Arguments', in *The Philosophical Review*, Vol. LXIX, No. 1, January 1960. Reprinted in *Religion and Understanding*, ed. D. Z. Phillips, Blackwell,, 1967.

——'Is it a Religious Belief that "God Exists"?' in *Faith and the Philosophers*, ed. John Hick, London, 1964.

Moore, G. E.: 'A Defence of Common Sense', in *Contemporary British Philosophy*, 2nd Series, ed. J. H. Muirhead, 1925. Reprinted in *Philosophical Papers*, Allen and Unwin, 1959.

——'A Reply to My Critics' in *The Philosophy of George Edward Moore*, ed. Schilpp, Evanston, 1942.

Mounce, H. O.: 'Self-Deception', *Proceedings of the Aristotelian Society*, Supp. Vol. XLV, 1971.

——'Understanding a Primitive Society', in *Philosophy*, Vol. 48, October, 1973.

Murphy, A. E.: 'Blanshard on Good in General', in *The Philosophical Review*, Vol. 72, 1963.

Phillips, D. Z.: 'Wisdom's Gods', in *The Philosophical Quarterly*, Vol. 19, 1969. Reprinted in *Faith and Philosophical Enquiry*, Routledge, 1970.

——'From World to God?', *Proceedings of the Aristotelian Society*, Supp. Vol. LXI, 1967. Reprinted in *Faith and Philosophical Enquiry*, Routledge, 1970.

——'Religious Beliefs and Language-Games', in *Ratio* XII/I, 1970. Reprinted in *Faith and Philosophical Enquiry*, Routledge, 1970.

Rhees, Rush: 'Some Developments in Wittgenstein's Views of
  Ethics', in *The Philosophical Review*, Vol. LXXIV, January, 1965.
  Reprinted in *Discussions of Wittgenstein*, Routledge, 1970.
——'Religion and Language', in *Without Answers*, Routledge, 1969.
——'Introductory Note' to Wittgenstein's 'Remarks on Frazer's
    Golden Bough', in *The Human World*, No. 3, May 1971.
Smith, Norman Kemp: 'Is Divine Existence Credible?', in *Proceedings
  of the British Academy*, 1931. Reprinted in *Religion and Under-
  standing*, ed. D. Z. Phillips, Blackwell, 1967.
Tennessen, Hermann: 'A Masterpiece of Existential Blasphemy', in
  The Human World, No. 13, 1973.
Unamuno, Miguel De: 'My Religion', in *Perplexities and Paradoxes*,
  New York, 1968.
Weil, Simone: 'A War of Religions', in *Selected Essays*, Oxford, 1962.
Wilson, John Cook: 'Rational Grounds of Belief in God', in *Statement
  and Inference*, ed. A. S. L. Farquharson, Oxford, 1926.
Winch, Peter: 'Understanding a Primitive Society', in *The American
  Philosophical Quarterly*, Vol. II, 1965. Reprinted in *Ethics and
  Action*, Routledge, 1973, and in *Religion and Understanding*, ed.
  D. Z. Phillips, Blackwell. 1967.
——'Knowledge and Practice', Unpublished paper on Simone Weil.
Wisdom, John: 'Gods', in *Philosophy and Psychoanalysis*, Blackwell,
  1968.
——'The Logic of God', in *Paradox and Discovery*, Blackwell, 1965.
Wittgenstein, Ludwig: 'Remarks on Frazer's *Golden Bough*', trans.
  A. C. Miles and Rush Rhees, in *The Human World*, No. 3, May
  1971.

Index of Names

Index of Subjects